The LIFE~GIVING POWER of HONOR

Unleash the Power that Can Transform Your World

Rob Packer

The Life-Giving Power of Honor

THE LIFE-GIVING POWER OF HONOR

© 2017 Rob Packer

All rights reserved. No part of this publication may be reproduced, stored in a retrieval system or transmitted in any form or by any means – electronic, mechanical, photocopy, recording or any other without the prior written permission of the author.

Unless otherwise identified, Scripture quotations are taken from the NEW AMERICAN STANDARD BIBLE®(NASB), Copyright © 1960, 1962, 1963, 1968, 1971, 1972, 1973, 1975, 1977, 1995 by The Lockman Foundation, Used by permission. www.Lockman.org.

Scripture quotations marked (NIV) taken from THE HOLY BIBLE, NEW INTERNATIONAL VERSION®, NIV® Copyright © 1973, 1978, 1984, 2011 by Biblica, Inc.® Used by permission. All rights reserved worldwide.

Scripture quotations marked (KJV) taken from King James Version. Public Domain.

Published by
XP Publishing
A Department of Patricia King Ministries
P.O. Box 1017
Maricopa, AZ 85139
All Rights Reserved

ISBN: 978-1-621661-327-0

Endorsements

The first time I heard Rob Packer teach on honor, I was in awe of the revelation. God loves honor and rewards those who walk in it…who live it. Rob Packer indeed walks and lives in honor. *The Life-Giving Power of Honor* will give you transformational revelatory insights and practical applications into the subject – you will be not only impacted but also empowered to embrace the qualities, benefits and rewards of godly honor.

>Patricia King
>Founder, Patricia King Ministries
>PatriciaKing.com

When a well-known international ministry told me that Rob Packer's teaching on "honor" was the best she'd ever heard, I determined to "sit up and listen" when he taught on the subject! I wasn't disappointed. Now, as Rob releases this book, I am even more impressed by his revelation on this essential value. He skillfully teaches on this subject from many angles to bring us into a whole new understanding and revelation of *The Life-Giving Power of Honor*.

Do we allow God to be Himself in our lives and our churches? Do we, ourselves, know what it means to be released and revealed? Rob Packer unpacks these key questions – key questions that need to be unpacked for the Body of Christ so she may enter her full destiny and purpose. Understanding the power of honor will release individuals, leaders and churches throughout the nations to enter into their destiny and purpose.

> Pastor Janet Chambers
> Living Waters Christian Centre
> Christchurch

Rob Packer is a legend in our nation. Over many decades, he has been involved with worship, songwriting, and leadership, and has consistently demonstrated integrity and the honor this book speaks about.

When I first heard Rob preach about honor, I was hugely impacted. I have heard many messages about this topic, but none carries the revelation that Rob has. Having recorded his message, I cheekily asked him if I may preach his sermon. He not only gave me permission, but his notes and PowerPoint presentation as well!

Growing up in a nation with a "Tall Poppy Syndrome," it was part of our national psyche to "cut people down to size" before they got "too big for their boots." This destructive trait reaped unnecessary suffering and extinguished potential. While I believe that the root to that has been dealt with, there is an urgent need to sow seeds of honor instead, which displaces residual dishonor. This book is a call for the laborers of the harvest, providing them with seeds to plant, so the fruit of righteousness may spring up with fresh vigor in our land and throughout the nations.

I highly recommend this book to you. As you embrace this teaching, it will enrich your life and the lives of those you encounter.

> Pastor Dayle Wright
> Invercargill Christian Centre

ENDORSEMENTS

Rob Packer did a teaching session on honor at our Revival School during 2014. I, along with all those present, received such a powerful new appreciation of the power and beauty of the heavenly principle and culture of honor. I have heard and read many Christian teachings on honor over the years, but nothing that came close to the way Rob presented it. Subsequently I have noticed a change in my personal life and the lives of others who have heard Rob's teaching. The culture of who we are as a family of faith has been enhanced and, also, the way we look at God our heavenly Father, ourselves, and others. Now Rob has expanded even more and wrapped it all up in a book so that we can all feast on the greatness of this principle of honor in a deep and reflective way. *The Life-Giving Power of Honor* can, and will, cause a revolution in the Church for those who embrace the fullness of the truth it contains, and who enjoy the journey of personal, and corporate, transformation that it offers us. It is a must have for anyone wanting to see heaven on earth.

Pastor John Steffens MNZM
Fiordland New Life Church

I have had the privilege of knowing Rob for around seven years now. In that time we have had Rob minister at our events and have had both him and his wife Lyn in our home. There is nothing more refreshing than people who embody the message they preach. Rob is one of those people. I have seen firsthand this message of honor outwork through Rob and impact the lives of those around him. Because we live in the same city, I am regularly hearing from other leaders about how they have been encouraged, empowered, and impacted by Rob. It is with great excitement that I endorse his book, *The Life-Giving Power of Honor*. Rob is one of the most gifted teachers I personally know. Because of this and his genuine love for God and people, I know that you will be encouraged and empowered to experience the amazing outworking of honor in, and through, your own life.

>   Josh Klinkenberg
>   Director, InFlame Ministries
>   Sounds of the Nations Global Director

The principle of honor has often been misunderstood or missed completely by the church. Having known Rob for many years, and witnessed his life, I know that he carries a deep revelation of honor. As you read his story and the stories of others, you will gain a deeper understanding of how the principle of honor is so necessary for our lives and for the communities we live in. Rob has clearly outlined what the Scriptures actually say about how God intended honor to operate in the Kingdom of God. He communicates the deep things of God's Word in easy to understand language. Rob is a great friend and father, and I know that as you read *The Life-Giving Power of Honor,* you will gain an abundance of wisdom and understanding on how to unlock blessing and honor in your life.

>   Pastor Lynley Allan
>   Catch the Fire, Auckland

Rob Packer has carried this message on *The Life-Giving Power of Honor* for years. It has impacted us and our culture so profoundly that we aim to have him share this message in our church once a year, and we include it in the curriculum of Revival School Aotearoa, New Zealand, every year. In his book he is able to go into even more depth in communicating the priceless significance and power of honor. He has captured an understanding of honor that I have never seen expressed by anyone else and it has become an invaluable treasure in our culture.

>   Benji Alexander
>   Director, Revival School Aotearoa
>   New Zealand

ENDORSEMENTS

The Life-Giving Power of Honor answers questions that people are longing to ask. With a fresh openness and down-to-earth practicality, Rob addresses where we live and the questions of worth that afflict our soul. While many books speak on the need to give honor, this book starts with our need to receive. Only when we have freely received can we freely give. This gem of a book helps us to do both.

PASTOR PAM WATSON
PURSUIT CHURCH, AUCKLAND

I have known Rob Packer for over forty years now. Throughout, he has always reflected what it means to be a man of honor as a worshiper of God, husband to Lyn, father to his family, and as a pastor. This book, *The Life-Giving Power of Honor*, contains the powerful principles and secrets he has discovered and embodies that will bless many, enabling them to accelerate into God's wonderful purposes and provision for their lives – whatever their calling or situation may be. I thoroughly commend it, and the author, to you!

ALAN STEPHENSON
DIRECTOR, JOSHUA FOUNDATION
ARUSHA, TANZANIA

Table of Contents

Introduction – 13

1. The Search for Value and Identity – 17

2. What God Says About You – 35

3. What Honor Does – 43

4. What Honor Looks Like – 57

5. The Bigger Picture – 83

6. The Most Significant Relationship of All – 97

7. Will Somebody Let Me Be Me! – 105

8. What the World Needs Now – 123

Conclusion – 130

Introduction

We are moving irrevocably towards the time in human history that the whole created cosmos is longing for. It is groaning for this, waiting in eager anticipation for it. In the midst of the suffering, upheaval, discord and shaking going on in the world, in the midst of the darkness that is increasing in the earth, there is a light that is growing brighter; there is a hope that is breaking through the despair. I believe that the world is starting to see the very beginnings of what it has always longed for... the emerging, the unveiling, the revealing of the sons and daughters of God.

> For the anxious longing of the creation waits eagerly for the revealing of the sons of God. —Romans 8:19

> "Arise, shine; for your light has come, and the glory of the Lord has risen upon you. For behold, darkness will cover the earth and deep darkness the peoples; but the Lord will rise upon you and His glory will appear upon you. Nations will come to your light, and kings to the brightness of your rising. —Isaiah 60:1-3

THE LIFE-GIVING POWER OF HONOR

There are many people in the earth who are disillusioned with religiosity, dissatisfied with merely intellectual Christianity, and who are desperately wanting to encounter a real God who meets people in tangible, undeniable ways. They know that there has to be more to life than what they've experienced so far. They have an inbuilt knowledge that they were born for greatness, that they are destined to make a difference in this world, and that they were born to be loved and celebrated, not just tolerated. Some of them have a personal relationship with Jesus, but most have not discovered Him yet.

Among those who already have a relationship with Jesus, there is a generation of people arising who are breaking free from the shackles of religiosity. They are discovering what God really thinks about them – they are finding out who they really are, and the truth is too staggering for words! They are the sons and daughters of God, members of the royal family of the universe. The God who spoke the galaxies into existence is their Father. Jesus is their elder brother. They have been invited to share in the relationship that Father, Jesus, and Holy Spirit have with each other. It is mind-boggling! It's wilder than anything they've been told before! It is by far the best news that they've ever heard, and they're believing it, acting in line with it, and starting to walk in the fullness of their inheritance. They're beginning to walk in the realities of the Kingdom of Light, bringing a manifestation of the love and power of heaven into the earthly realm.

Does any of this resonate with you? Does it describe something of the hunger in your heart? If it does, then read on, because you've been invited on the most outrageous adventure possible, with a God who is totally in love with you, and it's vital that you know about it.

INTRODUCTION

You really can make a huge difference in this world! The enemy, Satan, is very threatened by you. You are loaded with good things that God has given you that can impact the lives of those around you.

In this book you will learn about the power of honor and you'll discover how to build an atmosphere around your life that will result in a greater freedom for you to be the wonderful "you" that God created, that will allow others the same freedom, and that will enable God to be who He wants to be to you. As you journey through this book, my prayer is that you will be ignited with a fresh passion to run your race, whatever that means for you, to release everything that you have and are into the world around you, and to finish strong!

At the end of each chapter there are several Reflection Points. These are questions that you can ask yourself to help you apply the truth contained in each chapter. Better still, get some friends together and use the questions as the basis for a group discussion. You can meet weekly for several weeks and discuss one chapter at a time.

Chapter 1

The Search for Value and Identity

Every person on the planet has been wired by God to instinctively ask, and answer, two incredibly important questions. We cannot help but ask those two questions, and we cannot help but answer them. We may not ask these questions verbally, but we *will* ask them internally.

What are the two questions?

1. Who am I?
2. What am I worth? or ...
   What is it that makes me valuable?

There is an instinctive desire within each of us to know who we really are and to know what it is that gives us worth. While there may be many different things that we could look to in order to give us our sense of worth, there are four main ones that I want us to consider:

1. Value due to **Performance**
2. Value due to **Position**
3. Value due to **Character**
4. **Intrinsic value**

I want to start by considering #4 – Intrinsic value.

Intrinsic Value

What is Intrinsic value? It is the value that is placed on people purely and simply because of the One who created them. It is the value that God places on them because they are made by Him and made in His image. No other factors are needed, or relevant, and that value is given by God, not by people. It is there regardless of whether the person or other people acknowledge it or not.

What does God say about your Intrinsic value?

> "For what will it profit a man if he gains the whole world and forfeits his soul? Or what will a man give in exchange for his soul?" —Matthew 16:26

The word *man* is not gender specific but really means "person." The question is rhetoric. "What can a person give in exchange for their soul?" The answer is, "Nothing." There is no price that could be equal to your value.

> No one can redeem the life of another or give to God a ransom for them– the ransom for a life is costly, no payment is ever enough– —Psalm 49:7 NIV

What does this verse mean? It literally means that the Intrinsic value of *one* of us is worth more than the combined wealth of the planet! Seriously, you are of incredible value to God! There is no monetary value that could be placed on your life. You are irreplaceable! You are one of a kind. There is no one who has ever lived on the earth, is alive now, or who will ever live, who has your set of fingerprints, your eye print, your DNA. There is no one who has your unique combination of hopes and dreams, gifts and abilities, strengths and weaknesses – you are truly unique! And God wants you to celebrate your uniqueness and know that He loves you totally, and He celebrates you! You can't earn His love – He loves you because He made you, and He wants you to rest, secure in that love, and let it fill every fiber of your being and every moment of your days.

There is a problem, though. Most of us have not grown up with a strong awareness of our Intrinsic value. If you grew up knowing that you were incredibly loved by God and that you didn't have to do a thing to earn that love, that there was absolutely no pressure on you to strive and perform for acceptance, and you were totally secure in that love and nothing could shake it – you are one very fortunate and very rare human being! Because most of us have experienced a huge lack of awareness of our Intrinsic value, we will instinctively try to find our sense of value in other ways – most often through Performance, Position, or a combination of both.

VALUE DUE TO PERFORMANCE

We usually establish a sense of value from Performance at a very young age. As children we are continually experimenting, trying new things and discovering who we are and what we are good at. Our need to belong, and to know that we fit in with our peers and family, is very strong, and the affirmation that we receive, or don't receive, as a child has a very powerful impact on us.

I remember many years ago attending a conference in New Zealand where a world-renowned Christian writer from England,

Selwyn Hughes, was speaking. In the course of his message he told us about an incident that took place when he was about ten years old. His class had been given an assignment to write a short story for homework. The following day all the students handed in their short stories. When they began their class the next morning, the teacher said to them, "Good morning, class. I want to start the day by reading to you an example of an outstanding short story," and began to read Selwyn's story out loud. The affirmation that came from the teacher that day so profoundly impacted him that he said to himself, "This is what I'm good at! This is what I want to do with my life!" History is a testament to the impact that his life and writing has had on multiplied millions of people around the world. Among the many writings that he produced is a daily devotional called *Every Day with Jesus,* which is still being used globally, long after He has gone to be with the Lord.

You might discover that you are good at sports or music, or math or acting, and when you receive positive affirmation by those around you it can communicate deeply to your inner person, the real you, that this is what gives you value as a person. Is that a bad thing? No, not necessarily, because we all need to be affirmed and encouraged in what we are doing.

The challenge for us is that when we don't have an accurate sense of our Intrinsic value as the main indicator of our worth, we are likely to base our worth mostly on our Performance, and this can lead to major difficulties for us. If left unchecked, it can set us up to be driven by a need to perform in order to obtain acceptance – from others and from God.

Performance-based Acceptance

Performance-based acceptance is rampant in our society, and, unfortunately, it is also widespread within the church. So many

Christians labor under a pervasive feeling that they just don't measure up – in God's eyes or in the eyes of the church. This perspective is consolidated when teaching is given from the pulpit that basically says, "If you want to be the person God wants you to be, then you need to pray more, read your Bible more, give more, fast more, evangelize more, etc." Each of these things are valid activities in the right context – a relationship where we know that we are already loved and accepted – but as a means of gaining His love and acceptance? No!

Performance-based acceptance can be found in the home, too.

- When a parent only shows love and affection to their child when the child gets good grades in school, what message does the child receive? *"You are only of value when you perform well at school."*

- When a parent says to their child, "Why aren't you more like your brother?" what message does the child receive? *"You are only of value when you are like someone else."*

It is not just positive activities like art, sports, music, etc., that can bring us the affirmation we long for. If a young person finds that the main source of affirmation they receive comes from peers when engaging in negative activities such as bullying, theft, drug use, etc., they will often resort to those activities because their heart desperately needs to know what it is that gives them value, and the affirmation they receive from engaging in those activities is supplying the answer for them.

Does God Value Our Performance?

God created us with the intention that we would do good works as a part of our daily lives.

> For we are His workmanship, created in Christ Jesus for good works, which God prepared beforehand so that we would walk in them. —Ephesians 2:10

He loves the good things that we do! He delights in them, but He never intended that they become a means of earning acceptance from Him or from those around us; neither did He ever intend that they define our identity. He intended that our good works would overflow as a response to His unconditional love and acceptance, plus the knowledge of our Intrinsic value in His eyes.

In the 1980s my wife Lyn was instrumental in helping many people discover the power of prophetic dance. She taught seminars on prophetic dance, spoke at conferences, and danced prophetically as a part of her ministry. Unwittingly and unknowingly she drifted into a trap that most of us encounter – the trap of *confusing who we are with what we do*. At a particular conference that she was ministering at, the Lord spoke to her and said, "I want you to put your dance shoes on the altar." She responded, "But why? I don't understand. I can't." The Lord repeated this instruction to her several times over the next two days of the conference, and each time her response was the same. Finally the Lord asked her, "Why can't you?" and without even thinking about it, up from her innermost being came the reply, "Because it's who I am!" The Lord said to her, "That's why you need to surrender them. You must learn to be Lyn my daughter, not Lyn the dancer." As a response to what the Lord said, she took off her dance shoes and put them on the altar, and then she began a process of letting the Lord show her her true identity as a daughter of the King, completely independent of anything that she did for Him. It ultimately brought her into a whole new realm of freedom and confidence in her identity and in her relationship with the Lord.

THE SEARCH FOR VALUE AND IDENTITY

VALUE DUE TO POSITION

Why is it that so many of us as children dream of being superheroes, or see ourselves doing great exploits and achieving great things? I believe it is because God has put within each of us the instinctive knowledge that we were born for greatness; we were born for a high Position. As mankind, we have lost our original high Position through the Fall, but the echo still resonates in every human heart, regardless of whether we know God or not – we know that there must be more, and we are desperately trying to find what has been lost.

This can be a very frustrating process as we try all sorts of things that promise to fulfill us or lift us higher in life. But they don't give us what they promise. In the following verses the apostle Paul is describing a condition of our old nature before we came into relationship with God. He uses the phrase "deceitful desires."

> You were taught, with regard to your former way of life, to put off your old self, which is being corrupted by its **deceitful desires**; to be made new in the attitude of your minds; and to put on the new self, created to be like God in true righteousness and holiness. —Ephesians 4:22-24 (NIV)

He says that our old life was being corrupted, which means it was shriveling up or withering away, because of deceitful desires. What is a deceitful desire? It is a desire that promises you something it can never deliver. He is describing exactly what so many of us experience in life – a desire for something that promises fulfillment, satisfaction and significance, yet when we get what we so wanted, we feel cheated, disappointed and frustrated, because what we were anticipating and hoping for has once again eluded us.

Proverbs 13:12 tells us, *"Hope deferred makes the heart sick, but desire fulfilled is a tree of life."* The result of this process happening too many times is that our inner life shrivels up and our confidence and expectancy withers away.

Looking to Position for our sense of value can be seen many times in the corporate business world, where a person is always seeking the next promotion – and maybe treading on other people to obtain it – or being obsessed with becoming the CEO of the company. Is it wrong to want a promotion? No. Is it wrong to want to be CEO of a company? Not at all. So what's the problem? The problem can arise when what is internally driving the person to obtain those "higher positions" is the thought that, *"When I get that promotion, then I will be significant. When I become CEO, then I will have value."* It is a deceitful desire and it can never deliver what it is promising. Someone once said, "What a tragedy to spend your whole life climbing the corporate ladder to find at the end of your life that it was leaning against the wrong wall."

The same perspective can also be found, though, in the Christian community. *"When I get into full time ministry, then I will be significant. When I become a pastor, a prophet, an apostle or whatever, then I will have value."* We may get into full time ministry and work full time for a church or Christian ministry (not realizing that every Christian is in full time ministry for the Lord, wherever they are), and then wonder why we wanted it so badly because it can never satisfy the longing and desire for significance and value that we are feeling.

The problem is certainly not a new one. Check out the disciples' attitudes in Mark 9:33-34: *"They came to Capernaum; and when He was in the house, He began to question them, 'What were you discussing on the way?' But they kept silent, for on the way they had discussed with one another which of them was the greatest."*

There is such a tension that many of us experience, with this innate knowledge that we were born for greatness, combined with a lack of knowledge as to how to achieve it.

The Seesaw Mechanism

There is a device that many children around the world enjoy playing on. In New Zealand we call it a seesaw. In the USA it is often called a teeter-totter. It is a long, narrow board supported by a single pivot point located in the midpoint between both ends. There is a seat on each end and two children are seated on it, one child at each end. The child whose seat is lowest pushes upwards with their legs and this results in the child on the other end moving downwards. This is a classic illustration of how many of us function in relationship with others when our sense of identity is found in our Position. We know that we are supposed to go "up" and the only way we know how to get there is to put others "down." Because God has wired us to live out of our sense of identity and worth and out of the answer to the questions – "Who am I?" – "What am I worth?" – we cannot help but fight to protect anything that threatens our sense of identity. If your sense of identity is found in your Position, you will most probably not find it easy to serve others, to promote or encourage others, because to put others up means you will consequently be lower in comparison to them, and that is not a good feeling when you are insecure about who you are. When you are secure in your identity, you are free to lift others up, encourage them and promote them, because to do so doesn't threaten who you are. Your needs have been met, and out of your security and stability you can lift people even higher than you are, and be happy in doing it.

I remember an experience I had as a twelve-year-old at school. We were planning for a 5-day school trip to a bay in the

Marlborough Sounds, a beautiful area of beaches, native bush, and abundant fish and bird life, located at the top of the South Island of New Zealand. As part of the trip we would be studying the seashore and its creatures, and the bird life in the bush. In preparation for this, we were given the task of drawing a map of the area and noting the various landmarks in the vicinity. I had never been good at drawing and I was really apprehensive about doing this. I remember feeling pretty insecure about myself at school and not having a lot of confidence, and when I made mistakes the other kids in the class would laugh at me. To this day I don't know how I managed to do it, but I actually managed to draw a really great map, with the landmarks all done in different colors – it looked really good! I distinctly remember the feeling of satisfaction and confidence that I experienced as a result of that, and, as I had finished mine a bit sooner than some of the other kids in the class, I went round the class and began to compliment some of my classmates on how well they were doing with their maps. That was so unlike me! I would not normally have had the confidence or security within myself to do that. So what made the difference? The fact that my project had turned out well made me feel secure, and that gave me the stability to be able to encourage others in their work. If mine hadn't turned out well, there was no way that I would have encouraged others about their work, because it would have made them look better than me.

Proverbs 13:10 (KJV) contains a very insightful statement – *"Only by pride cometh contention."* It is interesting that it *doesn't* say "Only by pride comes disagreement" or "Only by pride comes difference of perspective." If you have nine people in a room, you are likely to have nine different perspectives on a particular issue. What is contention? It is the need to prove that I am right. So let's ask a question: "Why do I need to be right?" It is because my identity is found in my Position. To be wrong would mean a lowering of my position, and I cannot afford for that to happen. It means that the questions, "Who am I?" and "What gives me value?" have not been answered as God intended that they be answered.

What is it that causes one person to look down on another person and judge them because *they don't do things the way that I do*? What is it that causes one church to look down on another church and criticize the people there because *they don't have the revelation that we have*? It is the seesaw mechanism in play. There is no revelation that God has already made provision for the need for a high position to be met, and the only way to feel good about themselves is to put others down.

When God has met the need that you have, the need to know who you really are and what it is that makes you valuable, it won't matter to you whether you are in a position of prominence or a position of obscurity; you will just use whatever Position you are in to love people, serve them, and be totally secure in doing it!

How Did Jesus Handle Position?

> Have this attitude in yourselves which was also in Christ Jesus, who, although He existed in the form of God, did not regard equality with God a thing to be grasped, but emptied Himself, taking the form of a bond-servant, and being made in the likeness of men. Being found in appearance as a man, He humbled Himself by becoming obedient to the point of death, even death on a cross. For this reason also, God highly exalted Him, and bestowed on Him the name which is above every name…" —Philippians 2:5-9

Jesus had the highest Position possible – being equal with God – and He didn't count it as something to be held on to. Why?

Because He knew that His identity was not found in His position – it was found in His relationship with His Father, and in who the Father declared Him to be. Therefore He was able to empty Himself of His position and be found in appearance as a man, even humbling Himself further by becoming obedient, even to the point of death. When you really know who you are, and you find your identity in who the Father says you are, you will be able to be placed in whatever position obedience to the Father will bring you, and it will not threaten your identity.

Listen to what John says about Him:

> Jesus, knowing that the Father had given all things into His hands, and that He had come forth from God and was going back to God, got up from supper, and laid aside His garments; and taking a towel, He girded Himself. Then He poured water into the basin, and began to wash the disciples' feet and to wipe them with the towel with which He was girded. —John 13:3-5

Jesus knew where He had come from, He knew who He was, and He knew His relationship with the Father, and in that context He girded Himself and washed His disciples' feet. Amazing!

Value Due to Character

To many people, Performance and Position are the main indicators of a person's value… but Character? That's not nearly as appealing. It's important for us to realize that God highly values our Character. It means so much to Him.

There is a big difference between our character and our personality.

Our personality is related to the unique way that we have been wired, and through which we express ourselves. Some of us are more effervescent and bubbly, the extroverts, and some of us are more phlegmatic and easygoing – nothing seems to rock our boat, but it sometimes takes a bomb under us to get us motivated! Usually, apart from a major crisis in our life, our personality type doesn't tend to change much, but our Character is very different, and is being formed by the decisions that we make each day:

- You will decide whether you are a peaceful person or an angry person.

- You will decide whether you are a generous person or a stingy person.

- You will decide whether you are a diligent person or a lazy person.

- You will decide whether you are a punctual person or a late person.

- You will decide whether you are a faithful person or an unfaithful person.

- You will decide whether you are a truthful person or a lying person.

- You will decide whether you are an encouraging person or a critical person.

- You will decide whether you are an honest person or a dishonest person.

All of the above are Character qualities that are formed by the decisions that we make. God places a really high value on who you are, and who you are becoming.

> But the LORD said to Samuel, "Do not consider his appearance or his height, for I have rejected him. The LORD does not look at the things people look at. People look at the outward appearance, but the LORD looks at the heart."
> —1 Samuel 16:7 (NIV)

> The refining pot is for silver and the furnace for gold, but the LORD tests hearts. —Proverbs 17:3

ACCESS TO THE DIVINE NATURE

When we come into relationship with Jesus, we find that He is not wanting us to give our life to Him, but rather, He wants to give His life to us! He invites us to receive from His life in us, and when we do, our character begins to change to become like His. How awesome is that!

> But as many as received Him, to them He gave the right to become children of God, even to those who believe in His name, who were born, not of blood nor of the will of the flesh nor of the will of man, but of God. —John 1:12-13

He offers us His joy:

> These things I have spoken to you so that My joy may be in you, and that your joy may be made full. —John 15:11

He offers us His peace:

> Peace I leave with you; My peace I give to you; not as the world gives do I give to you. Do not let your heart be troubled, nor let it be fearful. —John 14:27

We even have access to His faith:

> "...and the life which I now live in the flesh **I live by the faith**

of the Son of God, who loved me, and gave himself for me.
—Galatians 2:20 (KJV)

We have access to the divine nature, which is the character of Jesus Himself:

For by these He has granted to us His precious and magnificent promises, so that by them you may become partakers of the divine nature… —2 Peter 1:4

Make no mistake about it, the enemy knows how valuable and important your character is, which is why he will try to sabotage it. His manifesto was openly revealed by Jesus in John 10:10: *"The thief comes only **to steal and kill and destroy**; I came that they may have life, and have it abundantly."* He is openly hostile to you, totally committed to stealing everything that Jesus made legally yours, and he wants to destroy your reputation and your influence for good in the earth. If necessary, he is willing to play the "long game." That means that he doesn't mind your reputation growing and your influence increasing; in fact, that can play right into his hand.

Most of us in Christian ministry are delighted when our ministry Performance increases. That may mean different things for different ministries. For some it may be that many people are getting saved, for others it might be the number of people getting healed, or being baptized, or falling under the power of the Spirit, or rescued from drug addiction – the list could go on. Often, when our ministry Performance increases, so does our Position in the Christian community. We start to get a reputation, and we may become known as the place where things are happening, where God is moving. We can often begin to interpret the rise in Performance and Position as a sign that we have God's blessing, that we have His endorsement of our ministry and, in many cases, we can be easily persuaded that the little Character issues that are slipping into our lives are not really *that* important because, after all, look at what is happening in the Performance area of our ministry.

That is exactly what the enemy is looking for. He would far rather wait a few years and allow us to have an increased influence in the Body of Christ and in the community, as long as we ignore the Character flaws that the Holy Spirit is wanting to address in our lives. Because when we leave them undealt with, and our lives are unguarded, that is where the enemy will get in. He will have us set up for a moral lapse or a ministry fall. And when a ministry leader falls, the more people that the leader has influenced, the more people will be damaged and hurt by the fall. Never sacrifice Character for Performance and Position – it totally is not worth it!

The World's Perspective

The world will tell you, "Who you are is determined by what you do and what position you hold."

God turns that right on its head and says, "What you do and what position you may hold will flow out of who you are!"

ooOoo

Reflection Points

- Which of the following four areas – Performance, Position, Character and Intrinsic value – contributed most to your sense of value as you were growing up? Why was that?

THE SEARCH FOR VALUE AND IDENTITY

- How do you feel when you read that your Intrinsic value is worth more than the combined wealth of the planet?

- Are there still any ways in which you feel that your acceptance, by people or by God, is based on how well you perform? What are some ways that you can change that?

- Have you experienced a time when you wanted something that you thought would really give you significance and value, and when you got it, it failed to do that? What happened, and why it did it fail to deliver what you hoped it would?

- Can you think of a time when you experienced the "seesaw mechanism" at work in your relationship with others? What happened, and how did it make you feel?

- To what extent do you experience "contention" in your relationships with others? Can you identify the "need to be right" in yourself or in others?

- "Your character is being formed by the decisions that you make each day." Do you agree with that statement? Are there any "character-making decisions" you are finding to be a challenge at the moment?

- In what way have you experienced Jesus' joy, His peace, or His faith in your life so far? How did you access that? What difference did it make in the situation you were facing?

Chapter 2

WHAT GOD SAYS ABOUT YOU

So far we have looked at the instinctive search that each of us makes to find our identity and our value. The Bible has a word for recognizing value – it is the word "'Honor."

Honor is the recognition of a person's value and the expression appropriate to that value.

In the Old Testament, written in the Hebrew language, the words "glory" and "honor" spring from the same root word:[1]

Kabod <3519> – *having splendor, dignity, reputation* ... which comes from the word *Kabad* <3513>, which means *heavy, weighty, rich, abundant, honored, glorious.*

In the New Testament, written in the Greek language, we have two words, "glory" and "honor" which have similar meanings:[2]

Honor [<5092> *Time* (Tee-may)] which means, *A valuing by which a price is fixed, honor by reason of rank.*

---
[1] Strong, James. 1890. *Strong's Exhaustive Concordance of the Bible.* Abingdon Press.
[2] Ibid.

Glory [<1391> *Doxa*] which means *Opinion, estimate, view, dignity, exalted state.*

If we were to ask any group of Christians the question, "Is it appropriate for a Christian to go around seeking glory for themself?" the resounding answer would be, "No. Of course not! A person doing that would be full of themselves." Like Billy Graham once said, the smallest package he had ever seen was a man wrapped up in himself!

As you read the following Scriptures, be prepared for some surprises, because it is possible that God may tweak your theology, just as He did mine.

Glory and Honor

> To those who by persistence in doing good seek glory, honor and immortality, he will give eternal life. —Romans 2:7 (NIV)

What!? God rewards us when we seek glory and honor? Yes, because He created us with an instinctive homing device that must find the price tag attached to us, that must find our true value, and He always intended that such would be found and answered in the context of a relationship with Him.

What about this next one?

> To them God has chosen to make known among the Gentiles the glorious riches of this mystery, which is Christ in you, the hope of glory. —Colossians 1:27 (NIV)

It is Christ in you that is your hope of you knowing the dignity, view, and exalted state that you were created for.

> But there is a place where someone has testified: "What is mankind that you are mindful of them, a son of man that you

care for him? You made them a little lower than the angels; **you crowned them with glory and honor** and put everything under their feet."... In **bringing many sons and daughters to glory**, it was fitting that God, for whom and through whom everything exists, should make the pioneer of their salvation perfect through what he suffered. Both the one who makes people holy and those who are made holy are of the same family. So **Jesus is not ashamed to call them brothers and sisters."** —Hebrews 2:6-8; 10-11 (NIV)

Jesus has crowned you with glory and honor – you may not know it yet, but He has! He has brought many sons and daughters to glory. He has brought us to that exalted state that He Himself lives in! Jesus is not ashamed to call you brother or sister. Think of that – Jesus is your elder brother!

But there's more.

For those God foreknew he also predestined to be conformed to the likeness of his Son, that he might be the firstborn among many brothers and sisters. And those he predestined, he also called; those he called, he also justified; those he justified, he also glorified. —Romans 8:29-30 (NIV)

This is an amazing Scripture.

Verse 30 says that *those He predestined, he also called*. The word *called* means "to be issued a personal invitation, to be called by name." Jesus knew you personally when He called you into His family and into His Kingdom. You were issued a personal invitation to join the family of the Godhead.

But it doesn't stop there. *Those He called, He also justified.* Most of us are not proud of the track record of Performance we had before we came to know Jesus. There are things we did in the past which we would definitely erase if we had the chance, if we could have that time again. I read a report a number of years ago where a psychologist was saying that the source for a high percentage of psychological difficulties that people experience in life can be traced to unresolved guilt. The brilliant thing is that, regardless of what our track record was, Jesus totally cleansed it, provided forgiveness for the wrongs we had done, and enabled us to stand before Him with absolutely no legal basis for the enemy to point the finger of accusation at us. We were totally cleansed and justified; we had a brand new start!

And there's even more. *Those He justified, he also glorified.* Do you know what that means? I looked up the meaning of the word "glorified" in the Strong's Concordance and other Greek Lexicons. The reference number in the Strong's Concordance is 1392. This is what it means: *To hold in honor, clothe with splendor, render it excellent, to cause the dignity and worth of some person or thing to become manifest and acknowledged.*[3]

That whole verse 30 package in Romans 8 means that Jesus called you by name, issued you a personal invitation to become a member of His family, totally forgave you, cleansed you, removed any basis for guilt and shame to stay attached to you, and gave you a completely new start in life. And, as if that wasn't enough – He holds you in honor, He has clothed you with splendor, He made you excellent, and He openly acknowledged your dignity and your worth! He is recognizing your value and He is consistently expressing that to you in so many ways. He is consistently honoring you. He will not keep quiet about you! He is ecstatic about you! He celebrates your uniqueness and He loves who you are, and He openly boasts about you to the heavenly hosts, to the angels, to the cloud of witnesses ... to anyone who will listen!

---
[3] Ibid.

He Delights in You!

> "The LORD your God is with you, the Mighty Warrior who saves. He will take great delight in you; in his love he will no longer rebuke you, but will rejoice over you with singing."
> — Zephaniah 3:17 (NIV)

The word "rejoice" in the Hebrew language is the word *gul*, pronounced *gool* and it means *to spin around under the influence of violent emotion!* The Lord gets so excited about you that He spins around with joy! Come on, you've got to get this. It needs to get on the inside of you! Jesus is NOT disappointed in you, He does not just tolerate you, He does not wish you were more like someone else – He loves you, He likes you, He celebrates you and He loves to just be with you and do life together!

Is this starting to sound like good news? I hope so, because it's the message that we desperately need to hear.

But it gets even better...

You're Already at the Top!

> "I have given them the glory [<1391>] that you gave me, that they may be one as we are one." —John 17:22 (NIV)

This is Jesus speaking to the Father, and He is saying that He has given us – that's you, me, and every other person who has come into relationship with Him – the same glory, the same dignity, the same exalted state that God gave Him. Whether you feel like it's true or not, whether you believe it or not, *you have been given the same exalted state as Jesus!* That's incredible! Amazing! That's "blow-you-out-of-the-water" revelation! Do you realize that if you are in relationship with Jesus, you actually cannot get any higher, positionally, than you are right now? It is impossible!

You are a member of the royal family of the universe, the God who spoke the galaxies into existence is your Father, Jesus is your elder brother! The only way that you could get any higher positionally than you are right now would be for you to become the Godhead – and that is impossible. Yes, you are eternal, and you will live forever, but you are also finite, and the finite can never become the infinite. You literally are royalty! Someone once said, "Why stoop to become a president?" The whole of the created cosmos is groaning and travailing, waiting in anticipation and longing for the time when the true royal family will be unveiled in the earth, because when that happens the whole earth and every created thing will get to share in the liberty and the freedom enjoyed and expressed by the sons and daughters of the living God!

In the second phrase in John 17:22, Jesus gives us one of the reasons why He did that, why He gave us the same glory, the same exalted state that God gave Him ... *that they may be one as we are one*. As we asked earlier in this book, what is it that causes one church to look down on another church because *they don't have the revelation that we have?* It is because the seesaw mechanism is in operation and they have no revelation of how God has already met the need for a high position by bringing them into the royal family of God. When you get that revelation, when you understand that you are totally loved, eternally secure, wildly celebrated by the One who made you, and you have the same exalted state as Jesus, you don't need to put anyone else down to make yourself look good in comparison. You already know who you are, and as you are able to receive the honor that Jesus shows to you, you are able to show that same honor to those around you. And that brings unity to people.

One more Scripture –

It was for this He called you through our gospel, ***that you may gain the glory of our Lord Jesus Christ.***
　　　　　　　　　　　　　　　　—2 Thessalonians 2:14

ooOoo

REFLECTION POINTS

Look at the following statements, one at a time, and for each statement consider: How real does it feel to you? Why is that?

- God has crowned you with glory and honor.

- Jesus is your elder brother.

- You have been totally forgiven of all your sins – past, present and future (you have been justified).

- Jesus is declaring over you your dignity and your worth, and He is revealing it for all of heaven to see!

- God is singing over you with such emotion that He spins around with joy over you!

- You have been given by God the same exalted state as He gave Jesus. You are already at the top, positionally!

Chapter 3

WHAT HONOR DOES

Here are 3 very important statements that will help us understand the power of honor:

1. When you are recognized and valued for "who you are" by another person, it causes a response in you – it releases you to be "who you are" to them.

2. When you value another person for "who they are," it causes a response in them – it releases them to be "who they are" to you.

3. When you dishonor a person, you shut yourself off from receiving who they are and what they have to give.

My beautiful wife Lyn and I have been married for 39 years. That's certainly long enough to know each other really well, but we are still discovering new things about each other and about ourselves. In the course of our daily life together, there are a number of things that Lyn does on a regular basis. Some of those things are:

- She cooks the most amazing meals.
- She washes the clothes.
- She does all the interior decorating of our home.
- She makes some of her own garments.

Here's the truth – **if that's all that I see in her**, if that's all that I will recognize and acknowledge about her, **that's all that she can be to me** in the context of our relationship. But there's far more to her than just those things that I mentioned.

- She is really prophetic.
- She loves to champion those who have come from difficult backgrounds, and loves to see them rise and take hold of their destiny.
- She is a dancer.
- She is a poet.
- She is an artist.
- She is a sculptor.
- She is an author.
- She is a teacher.
- She is a mentor.

Because of our relationship, I have the power to shut a lot of that down. If I had chosen not to acknowledge, recognize, or encourage those gifts in her as she was discovering them, but rather had discouraged and mocked her, it is quite possible that she may never have developed in those areas.

She also has the power to shut down a lot of what happens in me. Honor and dishonor are that powerful!

God has created the world to function in the context of relationship, and He knows that no relationship can blossom

and grow unless each person in that relationship recognizes the value in the other and expresses that to them, appropriately and consistently.

The Environment of Honor

This creates an environment of honor, where all the good things that God has put in each person can grow and develop because they are recognized, celebrated, and given room to operate. Then each person can be to the other all that they truly are.

My brother, Graeme, is an amazing artist. He does phenomenal portraits of animals and, even now, is branching out into new styles of painting scenes in nature. I remember when, over 20 years ago, he would come up to Warkworth, where we were living at the time, to attend some monthly watercolor painting workshops. He would come to our home at the end of each workshop, have a cup of coffee, and show us the painting that he had done in the workshop that day. On seeing Graeme's paintings, Lyn would consistently say, "I'd love to paint, but I could never do that!" After a few months of this, Graeme got sick of her putting herself down, and the next time he came up, he said, "I've paid for you to come to this workshop, so you're coming with me and we're going to find out what you can do!" She went with him that day, rather nervously and with some apprehension, but she came home from the workshop with a beautiful watercolor painting of flowers. Her face was just alight with joy and satisfaction. She said when she got home, "I didn't know that I could paint. I didn't know that ability was in me!"

It just took a little bit of nudging and a whole new world of creativity opened up for her, which has since blessed many people. She has had her paintings displayed in art galleries and has won some prizes in art competitions. She has even held her own exhibitions and people have been so moved when looking at some of her paintings and the poetry she put alongside them (telling why she painted them) that they have received healing for past hurts and have come back into a relationship with Jesus.

Imagine what could have happened if, when Lyn was considering taking art lessons, I had said to her, "What, you paint? Not likely. You can't even draw properly. You'd be useless!" That lack of honor and lack of encouragement may have been enough to convince her that there was no point in her exploring that skill set, and look what we would have lost and missed out on!

Here are another 2 really important statements:

1. Honor sustains the human spirit.

2. Dishonor wounds the human spirit.

Honor Sustains the Human Spirit

About 20 years ago I went through an extended period of time where I felt like giving up – not on life, but on the worship ministry. I had been involved in worship ministry and pastoral ministry for about 20 years at that stage. During the 1980s, our church in Auckland had hosted a National Worship Ministry Conference for a few years, and I was heading up the worship ministry there during that time. There was not a lot of training available on worship ministry in that season and we would have people from all over New Zealand come and spend a week at the conference being refreshed, inspired, and equipped to lead the worship ministry back in their home churches.

It was quite a number of years after those conferences that I realized that almost all of those who were leading worship in churches were younger, in their early 20s, and I was hounded by this unshakeable feeling that it was time for me to hand over the baton of ministry, gracefully retire and let the younger ones get on with it. It wasn't depression or self pity, it was just the feeling that I'd done my time. I was feeling somewhat emotionally depleted, too, which probably didn't help.

At that time I attended a conference, and I was just sitting there in my seat listening to the speaker, Pastor Brent Douglas, when I heard him say, "Rob Packer, are you in the auditorium? Will you please stand up?" I was caught totally unaware. A little embarrassed, I stood up. He then proceeded to say, "Rob, I just want to honor you for all that you've sown into the worship ministry in this nation. You've been a pioneer in the area of worship and, in a time when there weren't a lot of resources available to help people in worship ministry, you held the Worship Conferences that inspired so many people throughout the nation. On behalf of all of them I want to say, "Thank you!" The rest of the conference delegates applauded and I sat down again.

It is difficult to describe exactly what happened to me during the minute or so that it took for him to say those words. It was as though there was an infusion of Spirit-life being pumped into me. I went from feeling emotionally depleted and ready to bow out of worship ministry, to feeling like I still had value, I still had a purpose, I still had a race to run, there was still a place for me and I still had something to contribute! I honestly didn't think that something that profound could happen in such a short time, and all as the result of a few words being spoken.

I want you to know – honor sustains the human spirit! When you recognize value in a person and you express that to them appropriately, don't be surprised at the huge effect that it can have in their life. At the time of writing this book I have now been involved in worship ministry for over 40 years. I am 63 years old and a few months ago I accepted the part time position of worship pastor in our home church, Hope Centre, here in Tauranga, New Zealand. I am totally convinced that one of the key reasons I am still in worship ministry today is the infusion of life that God gave me through those words of honor over 20 years ago.

Dishonor Wounds the Human Spirit

What about the second statement above – *Dishonor wounds the human spirit*?

I want to address something that is prevalent in the Body of Christ and is causing us to limp along as a Body and be way less effective than we could be. There are many Christian husbands who have not yet discovered their true identity and value, and still have the seesaw mechanism in operation in their lives. Their value is often found in their Performance and in their Position in the home and in their church community. Then something quite threatening starts to happen – the man's wife begins to discover her gift mix and starts to grow in her ministry expression.

As she begins to rise in growth and development, what is happening to him (from his perspective)? That's right – he begins to go down in comparison. All of a sudden she is looking a lot more spiritual than he is, but he is the head of the home, the *man*! He can't have that sort of thing happening. (Remember, whatever threatens your sense of identity, you will always fight against.) So he begins to discourage some of the things that she is finding expression in. Instead of cultivating the atmosphere of honor in their relationship and celebrating his wife's growth and development, he is threatened by it, and so takes whatever steps he deems necessary to protect his position and reputation, while keeping his wife in what he feels is her place. So many of our women have been deeply wounded by dishonor, especially in their own homes.

They have been held back from blossoming into the beautiful, Spirit-filled champions they were created to be – because we, the men, have been threatened by them. This has to stop! Men, let's ask God for the revelation of His love and the truth of who He has already made us. As we come to receive what God says about us and His celebration of us, let us release our women to become all that God created them to be! We need all of them to be flourishing, growing and finding their place of expression and fulfillment in the Kingdom.

Another reason why many of our women are held back from fulfilling the destiny that is on their lives is because there is confusion as to the accurate interpretation of the Scriptures regarding the role of women. It is not the purpose of this book to look at this issue in depth, but I believe that it is imperative that we take the time and effort to understand more clearly what Scripture says about this.

Here are some excellent resources that will help you:

Books

- *Why Not Women,* by Loren Cunningham and David Hamilton
- *God's Feminist Movement,* by Amber Picota (foreword by Patricia King)
- *Half the Church,* by Carolyn Custis James
- *Jesus Feminist,* by Sarah Bessey

CDs

- "Women in Christ Arise," by Patricia King and Mary Audrey Raycroft
- "Women – Strong by Design," by Lyn Packer

Healing from Dishonor and Its Wounds

If you've been dishonored in life, looked down on, or treated badly by others, you can know healing. You can be set free from the pain and hurt of those things and you can learn how to walk in wholeness in Christ. In most cases, healing from emotional wounds is part miracle, part process; the miracle happens when we believe what Christ did for us, we receive His healing, and He takes away our pain. The process comes in learning how to keep, and walk in, that healing.

How do you do that? How do you receive His healing? The following list is not a formula, but it contains things that many people have found to be helpful and true as they have found their healing and wholeness in Christ.

- Believe that God loves you. Allow yourself to come into agreement with that truth and ask God to show you His love and give you revelation, understanding, and experience of it. It's not enough to just know it conceptually; you must know His love experientially, as well.

   ...that Christ may dwell in your hearts through faith; and that you, being rooted and grounded in love, may be able to comprehend with all the saints what is the breadth and length and height and depth, and to know the love of Christ which surpasses knowledge, that you might be filled up to all the fullness of God. —Ephesians 3:17-19

- Get to know His true nature and character. He is loving, kind, gentle, faithful, patient. He does not lie, and He will never abuse your trust in Him.

- Know that He loves you so much that He provided for your healing in Christ's work on the cross, that He wants to take your pain, hurts and sorrows from you.

Surely He has borne our griefs and carried our sorrows...
—Isaiah 53:4 (NKJV)

He heals the brokenhearted and binds up their wounds.
—Psalm 147:3

- Learn what Christ has done for you. Search it out in Scripture and then accept and take advantage of it. Accept it by faith, believe it, and begin to walk in line with it. See yourself as He sees you and honor yourself as He honors you – in attitude, speech, and behavior.

- Know that it is God's will for you to be whole. It is the devil's will for you to be wounded, sick, fearful and powerless. Dishonor and the wounding that comes from it are works of the devil.

For God hath not given us the spirit of fear; but of power, and of love, and of a sound mind. *—2 Timothy 1:7 (KJV)*

...God anointed Jesus of Nazareth with the Holy Ghost and with power: who went about doing good, and healing all that were oppressed of the devil; for God was with him.
—Acts 10:38 (KJV)

- Forgive those who have hurt you. Unforgiveness blocks the healing power of God and can open the door for a tormenting spirit to afflict you. In Ephesians 4:32 we are told, *"Be kind to one another, tender-hearted, forgiving each other, just as God in Christ also has forgiven you."* Forgiveness comes not just by operating will power and choice, but also by accessing the life and power of the healing, wholeness, and forgiveness you've been gifted – that is, in accessing the healer and forgiver who has taken up residence in you.

- Don't push down your pain or "harden up." Allow your emotions to be released. Otherwise, as medical science tells us, they will wreak havoc on you physically. Our body stores memory, not only in our brain, but also in our cells, and our cells reap the effects of that repressed emotion. It's okay to cry, to feel anger, and to express it. Release those hurts and painful emotions into His hands. Holding onto hurt, pain and fear can block the healing power of Christ from working in your life. Jesus said of Himself in Luke 4:18 (NKJV), *"The Spirit of the Lord is on me, because he has anointed me to proclaim good news to the poor. He has sent me to proclaim freedom for the prisoners and recovery of sight for the blind, to set the oppressed free."*

- Ask Jesus to remove the pain and to heal you. Ask Him to deal with the lies that the enemy has spoken over you, replacing them with truth.

- Receive His healing and find rest for your soul.

    "Come to me all you who labour and are heavy laden, and I will give you rest." —Matthew 11:28 (NKJV)

- Get help from others as you go through the process of healing. Go for counseling, ask for prayer, share with others who can walk with you through things. You don't have to go through this alone. Scripture tells us to love one another and to bear one another's burdens.

    Bear one another's burdens... —Galatians 6:2

- Stop listening to the enemy. Don't allow Him to speak lies of insecurity, unworthiness, woundedness, and guilt to you. Learn to recognize the devil's voice; take those thoughts captive and counter them with truth. This can be a process of dealing with the lies of the enemy as he comes back and tries to tell you that Jesus didn't really heal you, that you're not good enough for God to bother with, etc. Fight the lies with Scripture and the truth that God has revealed to you about yourself, His love, and His healing power.

Casting down imaginations, and every high thing that exalteth itself against the knowledge of God, and bringing into captivity every thought to the obedience of Christ.
—2 Corinthians 10:5 (KJV)

- Get to know who you are in Christ. Feed yourself on what God says about you. Believe what He says about you. Decree that over yourself. See yourself as God sees you.

- Learn to live from the truth that Jesus has revealed to you about who you are. Establish your freedom – follow through and make sure to establish yourself in your new freedom.

- Learn to cast your cares on Him.

Casting all your care upon Him, for He cares for you.
—1 Peter 5:7

- Spend time being loved by Him. Enjoy His love, revel in it, experience it daily. His love is what gives you life. He wants you to have an abundant, full and free life.

Will Somebody Let Me Be Me!

Not only are we each asking the questions, "Who am I?" and "What am I worth?" but we are also desperately looking for a person, or a group of people, who will accept us for who we really are. It doesn't mean they need to think that we are the best person they've ever met but that they genuinely accept us for who we are, warts and all! When we find a person or a group of people like that, there is often a big sigh of contentment that happens on the inside of us – "Aaah, I've finally come home!" We long to be free to be who we really are. **Our heart cry is, "Will somebody let me be me!"** Can you identify with that? We'll pick up on that longing a bit later in the book.

WORDS, ATTITUDES, RESPONSES AND ACTIONS

One other thing that is really helpful for us to be aware of is that in expressing honor to a person, we need to consider not just our **Words**, but also our **Attitudes**, **Responses** and **Actions**. We are not talking about flattering people with words that are nice but not necessarily true. We are talking about letting our words, attitudes, responses and actions be used to genuinely express their value. If I asked you the question, "If I said to my wife, 'I love you,' would she be blessed by those words?" what answer would you give? The most common answer would be, "Yes." But what if I gave you some additional information? What if I told you that my attitudes, responses, and actions had been giving her a very different message during the week? Would the words be sufficient? Ladies, I'm sure you would answer with a resounding "No way!" Words alone will not cut it! When we are talking about recognizing the value of a person and expressing that to them appropriately, we are definitely including words in that expression, but our attitudes, responses, and actions towards that person must give the same message in order for it to be effective. We will pick up on this truth, also, a bit later in the book.

WHAT HONOR DOES

ooOoo

REFLECTION POINTS

- Think of a situation where you were recognized and valued for who you are. What happened, and how did it make you feel?

- Think of a situation where you valued another person for who they are. What happened, and what was the response of the other person?

- Think of a situation where you were dishonored. What happened, and how did it make you feel? Have you received healing for the effects of that dishonor yet?

- Which of the steps that help with the healing process (listed in this chapter) have you experienced yet? Which ones have you found most helpful?

- Consider the following statement – "No relationship can blossom and grow unless each person in that relationship recognizes the value in the other and expresses that to them, appropriately and consistently." How do you see that dynamic functioning in your relationships at the moment?

- Have you found a person, or a group of people, who will accept you for who you really are? If so, what difference has that made in your life? Are there any people that you know that need that acceptance from you? How could you show it to them?

Chapter 4

WHAT HONOR LOOKS LIKE

HAVING EYES TO SEE

Every person's Performance and Character is very much tied up with how they see themselves. It is linked to their sense of Identity. Usually the reason for any negative behavior that we exhibit is because we are acting in line with who we believe we are. I once heard Graham Cooke make this statement, "For so long the church has been calling people _out_ on their behavior, when they should be calling them _up_ to their identity." I love that! That doesn't mean that we condone or encourage negative behavior, but it does mean that we can see further than just the behavior being exhibited, and recognize the incredible Intrinsic value of the person that we are relating to.

When you can see the Intrinsic value in a person and you express it to them in some way, you are calling to the real person on the inside, the person that God created, full of amazing potential, so utterly unique and treasured by Him, and very few people can resist responding to that! It was our Intrinsic value alone that caused Jesus to come to earth and die for us on the cross. We had no Performance, Position, or Character to warrant such a response from Him.

> So from now on we regard no one from a worldly point of view. Though we once regarded Christ in this way, we do so no longer. —2 Corinthians 5:16 (NIV)

I believe that Paul is describing in this verse exactly what we are talking about. It doesn't take a high level of discernment to recognize wrong behavior in people, but to see past the behavior to the value of the real person ... that takes a different set of eyes; eyes that Jesus can give you if you ask Him.

Honor in the Home

> Jesus made an amazing statement in the gospel of Mark:
>
> *Jesus said to them, "A prophet is not without honor except in his hometown and among his own relatives and in his own household."* —Mark 6:4

He said that the place you are *least* likely to find honor is in your own home, among your own people. Why? Often it is because we are so familiar with each other that we don't recognize each other's uniqueness and value.

You may have grown up with your brother or sister, mother or father, and spent lots of time with them over the years, but do you see them as a totally unique person with their own personality, gift mix, made in the image of God and with off-the-chart Intrinsic value? Or has their failure in areas of Performance clouded your perception so you don't see who they really are?

WHAT HONOR LOOKS LIKE

"Honor your father and your mother, so that you may live long in the land the Lord *your God is giving you."*
—*Exodus 20:12 (NIV)*

This is the first command in Scripture that has a specific promise attached to it – but it carries some inherent difficulties. What do you do with that command if your father was really bad in the area of Performance? How do you honor him if he abused you or neglected you in some way? The truth is, you may not be able to honor him for his Performance, but you can honor him for his Position – he is still your father. The same would apply in relation to a teacher or employer or any other person in a place of authority in your life who had not related to you in an appropriate way.

Sarah's story

(Her name has been changed to give privacy to her family)

"I have discovered that forgiveness is a vital key in being able to honor a person, or to honor God. As long as I hold unforgiveness in my heart, I will only ever be able to honor with my mouth, but my heart will be disengaged. God talks about this disconnect in Isaiah 29:13 where He says, *'...this people draw near with their words and honor Me with their lip service, but they remove their hearts far from Me, and their reverence for Me consists of tradition learned by rote.'*

"As a child I grew up in a family where I suffered many years of sexual abuse, the sort of abuse no child should have to endure. As you can imagine, that left a lot of emotional wounding in my life and a lot of unresolved issues.

"When I was a teenager I heard the good news that Christ died for me because He loved me; that was the first time that I ever recall being told that someone loved me. I became comfortable with Jesus loving me – after all, He was presented as either Lord or as my elder brother. The problem, though, came subsequently when God was presented as being a Father. In my thinking I knew what fathers were like; they weren't to be trusted, so for a long time I lived with the fear that somewhere along the way, God the Father would abuse any trust I put in Him and hurt me. For many years, while I could easily relate to Jesus, and acknowledge with my head that God was Father, I couldn't relate to Him as such. I said that I did, but my heart really didn't want to accept that relationship.

"I knew I should honor God the Father and love Him, but my heart was full of things that made that difficult. Unconsciously, and unknown to my rational mind, I blamed Him for what had happened to me as a child. One day, God faced me with that and showed me that I held an offense against Him in my heart, and had done so since I was a child. My initial reaction was to say I didn't know Him as a child, so how could I have held an offense against Him since then? He replied that all mankind is born with an internal knowledge that there is a God, and He showed that to me in Scripture (Romans 1:18-21). After wrestling internally and talking it through with Him, I came to a place of agreement with Him and repented of that offense. I had to choose to believe that He knew what He was doing when I was born, that His plans for my life were for good, and that He would work all that I had been through for my good.

"This opened a door for me to begin to develop a relationship with Him as Father, of being able to accept His love and to honor Him in a way that I had never been able to before. Now the relationship of trust that I've developed with Him as my Papa is so precious!

"In that process I had to forgive God for the things that I believed He had done to wrong me. It didn't matter that He hadn't actually done anything Himself to harm me, but in my eyes He had let me down by allowing others to harm me. So I had to forgive Him for those perceived hurts. Little did I know that this work in my heart would open the way for Him to begin to unlock all the pain from my childhood abuse and bring me to a place of forgiving my parents.

"As a child I hated my parents for the abuse I suffered at their hands, and even after I became a Christian I still harbored anger and hatred toward them for many years. I knew that I should forgive them, and I said the words many times, but the anger and wounds in my heart spoke louder than the words in my mouth, and ultimately nullified them. I had to come to a place where I could acknowledge the hurt that was at the base of the hidden anger and hatred, and deal with that before I could truly walk in forgiveness. So began a process of the Lord facing me with things, me looking squarely at them, and working through the issues that were there, allowing Him to bring reconciliation and healing to my heart. It took a while, but finally I was able to say, 'Those wounds are no longer there and I've truly forgiven.'

"It's not enough to say the words 'I forgive so and so...' alone; that just puts a 'Band-Aid' over the hurts. The wounds must be faced, dealt with, and allowed to heal, and when they do, forgiveness actually comes much more easily.

"My Mum and my Dad were not what I would call good parents, but now I understand the factors that were at play in their lives and the issues and hurts that they had that were unresolved, leading them to behave in certain ways. Understanding those things, and dealing with my wounds, was part of learning to be able to honor them. They are my parents, they gave me a chance to know life and ultimately, because of that, to know God. They're made in God's image and He loves them, and because of that I can honor them, despite their poor track record in parenting.

"I've discovered that honoring a person doesn't mean that you have to approve of their behavior, or even let them into a close relationship with you; it is about recognizing their Intrinsic value. They have value because God created them and He loves them. Honoring others is about learning to see with God's eyes and think with the mind of Christ. It is about being renewed in my mind, as it says in Romans 12:1-2: *'Therefore I urge you, brethren, by the mercies of God, to present your bodies a living and holy sacrifice, acceptable to God, which is your spiritual service of worship. And do not be conformed to this world, but be transformed by the renewing of your mind, so that you may prove what the will of God is, that which is good and acceptable and perfect.'*

"God wants us to be transformed into the image of Christ, who is the image of the Father (Romans 8:29; Hebrews 1:3). God is love and He wants us to become love, too. The world is crying out to know love. I was, too, as a child, and I know that I am no different from every other person on the planet in that regard. Can I encourage you – allow God to deal with the hurts that prevent you from truly being able to honor people. If you do, it will bring you into a place of such freedom, and it will open the way for you to honor those around you and, in doing so, to show them God's love in the way they long for."

WHAT HONOR LOOKS LIKE

Honor Your Children

Honor in the home isn't just one way, with children honoring their parents. Parents, you need to honor your children! Recognize the unique way that God has created them, and allow them to be who they really are. You may have had some dreams for your life that you weren't able to fulfill – becoming a doctor or lawyer, a professional sports person, or whatever. Please don't put pressure on your child to achieve that goal or fulfill that dream for you. Let them discover their own calling and encourage them to follow God's leading in their life – that's what will totally fulfill them!

Please don't compare them with their brother or sister. Celebrate who they *are*, don't focus on what they are *not*. Celebrate every attempt that they make to do something well, regardless of the outcome. Believe that they did their best and let them know that. When their accomplishments aren't what either they, or you, hoped they would be, pour your love on them! Tell them how proud you are of them – they need to hear that. Let them know that they are loved and celebrated regardless of what mark they got in an exam, or whether or not they won their sports game.

Listen to their thoughts, ideas and opinions – they are worth listening to! Their judgments and assessments may not always be right, according to you, but if you let them know that you are willing to learn from them, as well as wanting them to learn from you, you will earn their respect in a big way!

When you say that you will be at their school play, their sports game, the school prize giving, or their birthday party, make sure that you don't allow work pressures to cause you to break your promise. Your attendance and participation tells them that they are worth you sacrificing other things to be there with them, and for them.

Deborah's Story

(Her name has been changed.)

"My siblings and I had a rough upbringing. Our mum was a single mum who sacrificed her physical and emotional health for our survival. We were physically and emotionally abused and neglected, and some of our basic needs for food, warmth and emotional care were not met. This was a result of a poorly equipped mother trying to raise her kids in a country that was ravaged by poverty and war. Eventually, Mum began heavily drinking her sorrows away and at the same time expressing her pain and hopelessness in detrimental ways towards us, her children. As a result, all three of us missed some important developmental stages in our upbringing, which made it challenging to survive.

"As the eldest child, I had many parental responsibilities placed on me, and by the age of six I was taking care of my four-year-old sister and my newly born brother. I related to them as a parent for many years because I was taking care of their basic needs to the best of my ability, especially after our mum passed away at the age of 42. Although my taking a parental role was necessary, it certainly created a gap between my siblings and me. As they were growing up, they made choices that inflicted a lot of pain and suffering on themselves. Their actions hurt me deeply because it seemed like no matter what I did or said, nothing would persuade them to make good decisions.

"As the years passed, I found it really challenging to snap out of the 'parent' mindset that I had been forced to adopt. I specifically recall my relationship with my younger brother and how I always used to talk to him as to a little brother, even after he grew up. I would get angry at him for making bad choices and talk to him in a disrespectful and dishonoring manner. As he got older our relationship got worse. It hurt me deeply and, other than continuing to plead with God on his behalf, I did not know what to do.

"Meanwhile, I was working on my own personal development and coming to understand that "the world will change around us when we change." I was also reading books such as *Wild at Heart: Discovering the Secret of a Man's Soul* by John Eldredge, and *Running on Empty: Overcoming Your Childhood Emotional Neglect* by Jonice Webb and Christine Musello, as well as many podcasts and other personal development materials. As a result, the concept of the power of honor was becoming more clear to me, so I decided to experiment on my brother. I decided to treat him as a man who knows what he is doing, and to respect his decisions. I changed the way I talked to him, and I became an encourager.

"The change was phenomenal! Our relationship began to heal and we were able to spend more time talking and hanging out. At times he even opened his heart to me. We began to pray more together, and eventually he began to ask for my counsel. As time passes, I can see that he is making better decisions and growing in his walk with God. It is still a work in progress, but I am really encouraged by the change that my attitude of honor towards him produced.

"This experience has caused me to be more aware of my attitude towards people. To the best of my ability I now position myself to honor people regardless of their actions. I see more positive results in dealing with people by changing my attitude towards them than I do by trying to point out their failings."

Marina's Story

"More often than not, we are a product of our environment. It shapes our paradigms, our worldview, and our sense of identity, which in turn affects our choices and lifestyle. A healthy, nurturing and honoring environment in the early stages of our life will most likely position us for a good life. However, the opposite is also true.

"My childhood environment was damaging to my worldview and to my identity. Many years of emotional and physical abuse and neglect led me to believe that the world is a cruel place and I would never make it in this scary world. I would never amount to much. As I was growing up, I saw so much abuse towards women by the men around me that I learned that men could not be trusted.

"At the age of 14 I encountered God, and His love for me was the beginning of my journey toward healing – the healing of my mind, the changing of my worldview, and the discovery of my true identity. Shortly after that encounter I was removed from my home environment and was surrounded by people who loved God and were gracious and kind to me. I was a very troublesome teenager, but instead of receiving constant criticism I experienced undeserving grace and honor. That positive environment was nurturing the good in me.

"Over the years I have experienced many positive and honoring environments that have produced so much healing in me. What stands out the most, though, is receiving honor from men, which is the exact opposite of what I had previously experienced. I saw men being good husbands and fathers, as well as leaders of positive change in their communities and around the world. I witnessed authenticity, honesty, generosity, kindness, compassion and much more, and these men honored me with their words and their actions. As a result of being honored by men, I have received so much healing that my view of men has changed and I now have men in my life who are my mentors, leaders, friends, and some that have even been able to take on a role of father."

Honoring Our Elders

In much of our western civilization, we have removed the place of honor that should be given to those who are our elders. There is a prevalent mindset in our culture that expects people who are over 60 to retire from work, get their pension, play bowls, move to an "old folks' home," and wait to die. They have done their bit, they have had their day; now they should move over and let the younger ones do their thing.

This is such a strategy from the enemy! People in their older years often have the greatest time availability, the greatest life experience resource, and the greatest financial resources of any time in their life. Many great business ventures, inventions, literary works, and works of art have been produced by people in the age group of 60–90. People over 60 are entering their most productive years and, naturally, the enemy doesn't want them to be productive, fulfilled, visionary – think of the damage they could do to his kingdom!

We must change this way of thinking! What is God's perspective on those who are in the second half of life?

- **They deserve to be honored and recognized for being the wonderful people they are!**

    "You shall rise up before the grayheaded and honor the aged, and you shall revere your God; I am the Lord.*"*
    —Leviticus 19:32

- Their wisdom and life experience are invaluable to those who are following in their footsteps.

  "Please inquire of past generations, and consider the things searched out by their fathers." —Job 8:8

  "Is not wisdom found among the aged? Does not long life bring understanding?" —Job 12:12 (NIV)

- Their latter years can be their most productive years when they let the Lord sustain them and renew them!

  The righteous will flourish like a palm tree, they will grow like a cedar of Lebanon; planted in the house of the LORD, they will flourish in the courts of our God. They will still bear fruit in old age, they will stay fresh and green, proclaiming, "The LORD is upright; he is my Rock, and there is no wickedness in him." —Psalm 92:12-15 (NIV)

  "Even to your old age I will be the same, and even to your graying years I will bear you! I have done it, and I will carry you; and I will bear you and I will deliver you." —Isaiah 46:4

  Therefore we do not lose heart. Though outwardly we are wasting away, yet inwardly we are being renewed day by day. —2 Corinthians 4:16 (NIV)

LET'S DELIBERATELY SHOW HONOR TO THOSE WHO ARE OLDER THAN US.

- Show your respect for them in the way that you speak and act toward them. Treat them kindly – after all, you will one day be their age, and you'll still want to be respected.

- Let them know that they are valued for who they are, especially the very elderly who are often made to feel that they have no value and are no longer of any use to society.

- Look for ways that you can draw on their wisdom and life experience.
- Let them know that you value them and that you appreciate all they've done over their lifetime.
- Encourage them to keep moving forward, taking ground, pioneering new things.
- Make them a part of your life and your family. Take them out for coffee, visit them in their homes. Invite them to yours. Get to know them more.
- Let them know that they are still needed and they are valuable members of the family of God, with much to impart to us.
- Listen to their life story, find out the things they've done over their lifetime. Don't just look at them as they are now – they have a lifetime of experiences and learning to share. Find out about them.
- Find out what skills and abilities they have and look for ways that they can utilize them.

IF YOU ARE IN THE 60–90+ YEAR AGE BRACKET...

- We need you! We need your wealth of wisdom, life experience, and encouragement.
- We need to see you still learning and growing – it's such an inspiration to us!
- We need all the good things that God has put within you to still be released into the earth.

- Please don't look down on those who are younger than you; they are coping with a world that is increasingly hostile and competitive. Make it your aim to encourage them and minister to them.

- Teach us what you've learned; deliberately look for ways that you can minister out of your wealth of knowledge and experience. Start ministries, go on missions trips, or help with community projects.

- Be deliberate in reaching out to those around you who are adjusting to the changes that growing older brings; encourage one another.

- Pray for us; we need you to pray!

- Remember always, you still have so much to give!

Honor in the Church

Lack of honor can be a major problem in our church families. The church, global and local, is totally loaded with incredible people resources. God has given awesome gifts to EVERYONE. No one is excluded. That is a huge threat to the enemy, who knows what would happen if all the good things that God put within people were to flourish and grow and find expression in the earth. The kingdom of darkness would be decimated!

From Satan's perspective, this must be contained; he must keep a lid on it! He knows that the ideal environment for all those gifts, abilities and ministries to flourish and find expression is an environment and atmosphere of honor. If only he can get us to not recognize each other's value and worth, and withhold the expression of that to each other, he and his kingdom are safe. He is then free to do his work amongst us, unhindered.

How can we deliberately create a culture of honor in our church family?

- **Find out what God says about you** and how He really feels about you!

- **Become secure in your own identity** and don't become threatened by other people's gifts and ministries; instead, celebrate them!

- **Make room for people's gifts and ministries to have expression.**

- **Don't be jealous of others**, and don't compete with them.

- **Let others know how much you appreciate them** and that they are a gift to your church family and to your community.

- **Regularly recognize the ways in which people serve the church family**, especially for those whose service is behind the scenes. Many people serve in our churches and in our communities without ever being thanked for what they do.

- **Value people for who they are, not just for what they do.** As a worship pastor I know the degree of sacrifice that many musicians and singers make in serving their congregation week after week. If there are not many other musicians available to serve, some musicians may be on the roster every Sunday. I remember on more than one occasion saying to a musician, "I care more for you as a person than for the contribution you make when you play your instrument. You've been on the roster for several weeks in a row, and you need to just have some time with your family in the congregation. Take next Sunday off and just be refreshed." On one occasion that meant that we had our worship time without a bass guitar, which was a sacrifice, but it meant that our bass player could have a rest from ministry.

- **Recognize that many people's gifts and ministries may not be expressed within the church context.** When a leader teaches from the pulpit that the main gifts of value are preaching, teaching, pastoring, and prophesying, they put a stumbling block in the way of the majority of the congregation. A very small percentage of the average congregation have preaching, teaching and pastoring as their main ministry. What about those who are gas station attendants, school teachers, checkout assistants, accountants, nurses, drain layers, driving instructors, police personnel...? The list could go on and on! We must equip them to be who they are called to be in their sphere of influence.

- **Senior leaders – your job is not to use your congregation to help accomplish your vision.** Your job, according to Ephesians 4:11-12, is to work with other five-fold ministries to equip the people of God for the work that He has called them to, to help give them wings and fulfill the vision that God has put in their heart.

And He gave some as apostles, and some as prophets, and some as evangelists, and some as pastors and teachers, for the equipping of the saints for the work of service, to the building up of the body of Christ. —*Ephesians 4:11-12*

- **Leaders – teach your people about Grace** – not greasy grace as a license to sin, but New Covenant biblical grace which empowers them not to live a lifestyle of sinning. It is the grace which lifts from them the burden of Performance-based acceptance and helps them to know and experience how incredibly loved they are, and celebrated by God. It helps them realize they are already made righteous by receiving His gift of righteousness, and they now get to learn how to live out of that righteousness. It's no longer about giving, fasting, or serving to gain God's approval, but rather it is about living and serving out of the approval and acceptance they already have!

...much more those who receive the abundance of grace and of the gift of righteousness will reign in life through the One, Jesus Christ. —Romans 5:17

- **Make your church culture one where it is totally safe for people to try new things**, make mistakes, and be totally supported, encouraged, and celebrated!

A young lady we know attended a Christian Training School, and during her time there she did something she knew was wrong. It came to the attention of the pastoral team of the school and she was asked to meet with a couple of the pastors. Her heart sank as she knew what was coming – she would be severely reprimanded and made to pay in some way for what she had done. That was what had happened every other time she had been disciplined in church life. The time came for her to meet with the pastors and she walked into their office and sat down. One of the pastors opened the conversation by relating the event that had come to their attention and then checked that their information was indeed correct. When the young lady confirmed that it was true, the pastors said, "This is what you did, but that is not who you are." Over the next hour or so they proceeded to speak over her what they saw in her and who she was in God's eyes, and spoke prophetically over her, calling to the real person inside and to the destiny that she had. By the end of her time with them she felt so built up, so encouraged and inspired, with a fresh vision of who she really was, that there was no way she was going to continue acting the way she had. She had just been called up to her identity!

Benji's story

"I have experienced two profoundly significant encounters with honor that have impacted me dramatically. One was in the context of position, the other in the context of the prophetic.

"Earlier in my life I had experienced several dysfunctional church contexts that had been both dishonoring and abusive. They hadn't held me back from pursuing the call of God on my life, but the most positive way I could describe them is 'character building.' However, when I met my current pastor, things were completely different! Instead of him being threatened by the calling on my life and shifting me sideways, or trying to control me or remove me, he promoted me. He recognized the calling on my life and placed me in a position of honor. It was especially powerful to me because I had never experienced so much kindness, generosity, humility and honor from a leader before. In fact, the level of honor he placed on me was borderline excessive. I felt deeply, deeply encouraged. He had championed me in a way that no one ever had before, and it was fuel to my fire. I rose to the challenge of the position, which demanded that I mature, grow, train, and develop fast – but I thrived! I grew immeasurably more in the context of borderline excessive honor than I ever could have dreamed of in the character building context of dysfunction.

"The second experience has been a repetitive experience. An internationally respected prophet, who is a mentor and friend of mine, has been prophesying over my life for years. She declares such greatness over me that I am in wonder at the possibility of ever walking in the fulfillment of the words that come out of her mouth. But as I have meditated on these words that she keeps declaring over me, two specific things have taken place.

"1. I am agreeing with those words more and more. My personal understanding of my identity and calling has been upgraded and lifted higher than anything that I had ever previously entertained. I see myself as becoming a great revivalist – that impacts me day after day, moment after moment. It impacts how I think and feel about myself (I feel awesome about myself, by the way!) It impacts how I dream, how I work; it impacts the atmosphere around my life. I'm going to write history and I'm now fully persuaded of it!

"2. The second thing that I've noticed is that these prophetic words that mirrored the perspective of the Father over my life are not just words bouncing around the cosmos now. They are becoming flesh in me. They are coming to pass and I am becoming a manifestation of what was spoken over me in honor and love. My life is literally completely different. Those prophetic words spoken in honor and love forged me as much as a blacksmith would forge a weapon with flames and an anvil.

"The Lord used the acts of honor of both of my friends to shape me, forge me, promote me and unleash me to pursue the fullness of what He has for me in ways that I could never have done independently."

Honor in the Marketplace

"Honor all people, love the brotherhood, fear God, honor the king." —1 Peter 2:17

Peter instructs us to honor *all* people. What about the drug addict or the street kid who probably has very little Performance, no Position, and possibly little in the way of Character to recommend them? How do you honor a person like that? You honor them for their Intrinsic value, which is off the charts!

JESUS AND ZACCHEUS

The account of Jesus meeting with Zaccheus in Luke chapter 19 is very powerful. There is so much going on in this encounter that just a superficial glance may not reveal. The Jews at that time were under the rule of Rome, and Rome imposed taxes on the Jews. The Roman leaders chose certain Jewish citizens to collect these taxes from their fellow countrymen, and they were encouraged to extort as much as they could from their own people by overcharging them and often making false charges of smuggling against them in the hope of extorting hush-money. They detained, and they opened letters on mere suspicion. It was the basest of all livelihoods, and tax collectors were regarded as traitors and apostates, willing tools of the oppressor, the lowest of the low! They got super rich at the expense of their own people. Zaccheus was not just a tax collector, he was a *chief* tax collector! He was responsible for coordinating the activities of other tax collectors and, as such, was loathed by the general populace.

Into this situation comes Jesus, totally aware of Zaccheus' poor Performance, his Position as the lowest of the low, his lack of Character. It seems Jesus is not put off by any of it. He knows these things about Zaccheus, but He's not concentrating on them at all.

Zaccheus has obviously heard much about Jesus, and perhaps has even seen some of the miracles that He's performed. Something is stirring in his life and he needs to find out more about this man who is turning society and the religious system of the time upside down! He is stirred so much that he pushes past the crowd and climbs a tree just to get a glimpse of Jesus, maybe to hear something that He will teach the crowds, maybe to see another miracle take place.

And then Jesus does something extraordinary. He looks up at Zaccheus, seeing past the deficiencies in his life, seeing past the betrayal of his countrymen, seeing past the contempt that he was held in by his own people, and sees his Intrinsic value. He sees the real person on the inside, and in one expression of honor He calls to the real Zaccheus and shows him what He thinks of him. He says, *"Zaccheus, hurry and come down, for today I must stay at your house." (Luke 19:5)*

Boom!! It sent shock waves through the entire crowd! No one was expecting this. Not Zaccheus! Not this low life! Surely Jesus knew who this man was, and yet He accorded him a place of honor that many of the religious leaders in the crowd would have loved to have had – having Jesus at their home!

What is interesting and very significant is what Jesus *doesn't* do. He doesn't confront Zaccheus with his obvious wrongdoing. He doesn't berate him for the stealing of money from his own people. He just, in effect, says, "I want to hang out with you. You're important to Me and you're important to My Father."

This so profoundly impacted Zaccheus, who knew all the wrong that he had done, that he responded by doing something that Jesus hadn't even talked to him about – he said, *"Lord, half of my possessions I will give to the poor, and if I have defrauded anyone of anything, I will give back four times as much." (Luke 19:8)* Wow! It is the kindness of God that leads us to repentance (Romans 2:4).

Night Markets

When we lived in Auckland as a part of the XP Ministries outreach there, our friends Andrew and Erin Bradley headed up a ministry at the Pakuranga Night Markets. Every Saturday night, an indoor car park in Pakuranga was turned into a Night Market where all sorts of foods and crafts were sold. Every second Saturday night from 6:00 p.m. till 11:00 p.m. we had a stall there with a banner advertising Free Dream Interpretations, Free Spiritual Readings (Words of Knowledge), Free Destiny Words (Prophetic Words), Free Spiritual Cleanse (Deliverance), Free Spiritual Encounter (where we would pray for the Holy Spirit to touch people with His love), Free Healing Prayer (we would pray for physical or emotional healing), Free Tattoo Readings (where we would ask Holy Spirit for insight into the meaning of any tattoos that people had on their body, and then give a prophetic word which would spring off the meaning that He gave us.) When people came into our stall, we would explain that we weren't psychics but that we were Christians who believed that God wanted to speak encouraging things to us about our lives, and wanted people to experience His love in tangible ways. I don't remember anyone walking out when they heard that we weren't psychics. People everywhere are hungry for spiritual reality, and they are longing for encouragement in their life journey. Our goal was not to ram the gospel down their throat, but to hear God's heart for them, speak what He told us to say, and see how the person responded. Whether we got to introduce them to Jesus or not would be determined by whether or not they wanted it at that point in their journey.

We had many people who were healed instantaneously of injury, pain, and sickness. One of the managers of the Night Market had an injured arm, one of our team prayed for him, and he felt something in his arm at the time when he was prayed for, but it wasn't healed right then. When he woke up the next morning his arm was free from pain and he had complete freedom of movement restored to his arm. He was so ecstatic about it that for many Saturday nights after that he would tell all the other stall owners, "If you have any sickness or pain, go and see those people in the Dream Interpretation stall. They'll fix you up!"

Erin and Andrew, who also have a ministry helping people with Dream Interpretation, had the privilege of showing many people what God was saying to them through their dreams. There would also be people who just wanted a Spiritual Encounter. One lady, who was in a very stressful situation in her life, was prayed for by one of our team. He just prayed that Holy Spirit would come and touch her with His peace. She began to encounter Him and He filled her with such a powerful sense of His presence and peace that she just sat there in the chair, with her hands outstretched, for about 20 minutes. People everywhere are spiritually hungry, and we found that one of the things that would most effectively enable them to open up and receive from God, even when they didn't know anything about Him, was to be loved, accepted and honored for who they are.

What are some other ways that we can show honor to people?

- Celebrate who they are, rather than focusing on who they are not.
- Resist comparing them with yourself or others, because they are totally unique. Celebrate their uniqueness!
- Speak to them with kindness, not with sarcasm or mockery.

- Give them your full attention when they are talking to you. They are worth it!

- In the midst of your busyness, take time to listen to them.

- When someone makes a mistake, assume that they meant well and that they did their best. Give them the benefit of the doubt until you are forced to do otherwise.

- Acknowledge their presence when they are with you. No one likes to feel invisible.

- Thank them for what they do and for the difference they are making. You can do this for your waiter at the restaurant, the cleaner sweeping the streets, the people who collect your garbage, the attendant at the gas station, the checkout operator at the supermarket, the people who serve in your local church – there are so many people who make a huge difference in our society but are very seldom thanked for what they do.

- Notice the appearance of someone that you meet and compliment them genuinely on how they look.

- Buy a coffee, or pay for the groceries, for the person behind you in the queue.

- Look for something good about the person you are meeting with; tell them you appreciate who they are and what they do.

- Take only the allotted time for lunch at work and don't steal the boss' time.

- Do the best that you can at your place of work, regardless of how menial your tasks may be, and do your work with joy.

- Open the door for someone and let them go first.

- In a traffic queue, let someone from a side street in ahead of you.

- Visit a person who is older than you and ask them to share something that they've learned in their life's journey.

- Encourage someone who is younger than you regarding something they are doing, and show them you support them.

ooOoo

Reflection Points

- Think about any people you know who exhibit negative or unhelpful behavior. In what way are they acting in line with who they believe that they are? What are some ways that you could help them to see their real Intrinsic value?

- Think about your family – your brothers or sisters, your mother and father. Is honor functioning in your relationship with them? If not, what would be one practical step you could take to express honor to one of your family members?

- Think of the people you know who are quite a bit older than you. Do you know anything of their life story? What could you learn from their experiences that would be helpful to you? Are they active and productive, or do they feel that they are no longer needed? If they feel that they're no longer needed, how could you help to change their perspective?

- If you are in the over-60s age group – what younger people do you know who would really love to have another Mum or Dad figure in their life, another Grandpa or Grandma to help and encourage them? What experiences could you share with others to encourage them in their journey? What skills and abilities do you have that you are not currently using? In what ways could you put them to use to be a blessing to those around you? What new skills would you like to learn? Who could you learn them from? Think of something you've always wanted to do but never got around to doing. What is one step you could take to begin making that a reality?

- Is there anyone in your church family that you compare yourself to? How does that comparison make you feel? What does that comparison tell you about who you see yourself to be?

- Who do you know that is doing a regular act of serving behind the scenes without being in the limelight and without much recognition from others? In what ways could you show them how much you appreciate who they are and what they do?

- What difference would it make in your church family if, instead of calling people *out* on their behavior, you called them *up* to their identity?

- Think of some of the people you know in your church family. What are their gifts and abilities, and how could you deliberately make room for them to flourish and grow? What could you do that would let them know they are loved and celebrated?

- Think of some of the people you know who don't yet have a relationship with Jesus. What are some ways you could let them know that they are loved and celebrated exactly as they are? Can you relate to them without judging them, and take time to listen to their story?

Chapter 5

THE BIGGER PICTURE

We've seen so far how the power of honor works in relationship between people, but there is a bigger picture here. The relationships that we have with one another are actually microcosms of a much bigger, much more powerful relationship – the relationship between God and His people.

We looked in chapter 3 at the truth that, "*When you are recognized and valued for 'who you are' by another person, it causes a response in you ... it releases you to be 'who you are' to them.*" We looked at the fact that every one of us has a longing to be accepted for who we are, and we experience the heart cry, "Will somebody let me be me!"

Why are we like this? Where did we get those longings from? Well, whose image are we made in? God's. *We are like this because He is like this. He wants to be accepted for who He is.*

Have you ever wondered, "Why does God want worship?" Does He have an unstable ego that loves to have people bowing down before Him so that He can feel so much better about Himself? Not at all! As we mentioned earlier, God created the universe to function in the context of relationship because He is a relational being and He knows that **no relationship can flourish and grow unless each party in that relationship recognizes the value of the other, and expresses that to them, appropriately and consistently.** That environment of honor is exactly what the relationship needs for it to grow into its fullness – each person being able to be exactly who they are to the other.

If the truth that *when you are recognized and valued for 'who you are' by another person, it releases you to be 'who you are' to them* is powerful, and it is, then this next truth is mind-blowingly explosive in its implications…

When you recognize and value God for 'who He is,' and express that appropriately to Him, it causes a response in Him – it releases Him to be 'who He is' to you!

When it comes to relationship with God, worship is one of the most natural ways of expressing to Him His worth and value. Worship is way more than just singing songs – it is a lifestyle of responding to, and expressing, the wonder of who He is and what He has done. The whole point of worship is that it focuses on God, not us; it focuses on His worth and the wonder of who He is, not on our inadequacies and failures. When we express to Him what He means to us, it honors Him and releases Him to be Himself to us. God has invited us into a vibrant, pulsing-with-life relationship with Himself, where we not only express our love to Him but where we expect Him to respond to us. We also expect to engage with Him in real and unmistakeable ways; we expect Him to reveal more of Himself to us, and we expect to have genuine encounters with Him that transform us in the process!

What Sort of God is He?

One of the heart cries of God is, "Will somebody let Me be Me!" So what sort of God is He? Let's consider who He is, and His value, in the context of the four major areas we identified at the beginning of this book:

VALUE DUE TO PERFORMANCE

Creation – You only have to look at the vastness of the night sky, the position of the earth in relation to the sun and moon, the intricacy and design of flowers, the incredible variety of plant, bird, insect and animal life, the colors in a sunset, the mechanism of sight and hearing, the complexity of the brain, the things that we are discovering about the sub-atomic and quantum realm, and the many facets of the spirit realm to realize the amazing complexity of creation! God is a genius at what He does!!

The Cross – What Jesus accomplished through His death and resurrection is astounding! He totally destroyed Satan's hold over mankind, He plundered hell, secured the keys of hell and death, and rose forever triumphant, having secured salvation and freedom and making them available to all people! It is by far the most effective rescue mission ever staged in human history.

The Jewish Nation – The Jewish nation is an enigma when it comes to people groups. No other nation has been dispersed among the other nations of the world for thousands of years and still retained its national identity. No other nation has been called by God as Israel has, and has been promised that God would bring them back to their own national land and restore their national sovereignty, and yet God did it with Israel, and in 1948 they returned and established the nation again.

Miracles in Scripture – Consider the number of times that God stepped into the natural course of events in human history and did something remarkable but totally outside of man's ability:

- The burning bush
- The plagues in Egypt
- The parting of the Red Sea
- The walls of Jericho
- The parting of the river Jordan in flood season
- Manna from heaven
- Water from the rock
- The pillars of cloud and of fire
- The donkey that spoke
- Fire from heaven that consumed the wood and the altar
- The axe-head that floated
- The jars of oil that kept replenishing
- A child brought back from the dead
- Leprosy being cured by dipping in the Jordan river
- The sun standing still for a day
- The miracles of Jesus
- The resurrection of Jesus … and we could go on and on.

Prophecies Fulfilled – There are many prophecies given in Scripture that came true, many of them hundreds of years after they were given. They were insights received from another realm. The dream that Nebuchadnezzar had of the statue that represented the kingdoms to come after him, the prophecy of Israel's time in Egypt and subsequent deliverance, the prophecies of the dispersion and the re-assembling of the Jewish nation, the prophecies of the coming Messiah, which told that He would come from Bethlehem, that He would come out of Egypt, that He would conquer, that He would suffer and die, that He would ride on a donkey. No wonder the leaders of the Jews could not figure this all out, because it was so diverse, yet in looking back, all of those prophecies, and more, were fulfilled in Jesus.

People in Scripture – As you read through Scripture, you find hundreds of accounts of people's genuine encounters with the living God. The encounters often included miracles of provision, healing or deliverance, but they also included times when they received wisdom, comfort, and instruction on how to live well. As you read through these accounts, you will see how frequently God engages with His people and how He loves and supports them at all times, even when correction is needed.

People You Know – Let's bring this a little closer to home. Think of the people you know, and the testimonies you've heard of their answers to prayer, encounters with God, lives filled with His peace and joy. God has been active in every one of those people and He's still working in them.

Your Own Life – Now right onto home base … your own personal track record of answered prayer, times of meeting with God, hearing His voice and receiving His love.

God scores top marks for Performance!!!

VALUE DUE TO POSITION

He is the...

- **Creator of all** – Everything was made through Him and for Him. (Colossian 1:16)

- **Source of all things** – Everything originates in Him. (Isaiah 44:24)

- **Sustainer of all things** – Everything derives its life from Him, and in Him all things are together. (Colossians 1:17)

- **Owner of all things** – By virtue of the fact that He has created everything. (Psalm 50:12)

- **Judge of all** – Everyone is ultimately accountable to Him for how they live. (Acts 17:30-31; 2 Corinthians 5:10)

- **God Almighty** – There is nothing that is too hard for Him. (Jeremiah 32:27; Matthew 19:26)

- **Head of the Armies of Heaven** – There are multitudes of angelic beings at His command. (Matthew 25:31; 26:53; Revelation 19:11-16)

- **Head of the Body of Christ** – It is His Church, not ours. He has bought it with the blood of Jesus. (Colossians 1:18)

- **King of all the nations** – He is the King of kings and ultimately every national ruler is accountable to Him. (Psalm 72:11; 86:9; Revelation 17:14; 19:15-16)

- **Father from whom every family derives its name** – He is the ultimate Father; He loves His children! (Ephesians 3:14-15)

You can't beat that in terms of position. He has the highest position of all!

Value due to Character

He is...

- **Pure** – There is no defilement in Him, He is without shadow or variation, He is flawless. (Deuteronomy 32:4; James 1:17)

- **Righteous** – He has total integrity; every decision He makes is right and perfect for the situation. (Deuteronomy 32:4; Psalm 18:30; 89:14)

- **Love** – He is not just loving, but He *is* love – it is the essence of who He is. He is always choosing the best for His creation. (John 3:16; 15:9; 17:26; Romans 5:8)

- **Faithful** – When He says something, He will do it. He can be totally relied on to do what He has promised. (Numbers 23:19; Deuteronomy 32:4; Psalm 33:4; 36:5; Hebrews 13:5-6)

- **True** – He is absolute Truth, He never lies, and what He says can be trusted, believed, and acted on. (Numbers 23:19; Psalm 57:3; John 1:17; 14:6)

- **All knowing** – He knows all things and nothing escapes His notice. He has total wisdom and understanding. (Romans 11:33,34; Colossians 2:2,3; Hebrews 4:13)

- **Generous** – He is extravagantly generous, and He wants to be that *to* you, and *through* you. (Psalm 145:14-19; John 3:16; 2 Corinthians 8:9)

- **Healer** – He loves to heal people; there is nothing that He can't heal. (Exodus 15:26; Psalm 103:3; 107:20; 1 Peter 2:24)

- **Deliverer** – He loves to set people free, and there is no bondage that He can't break! (Isaiah 60:1-3; Psalm 32:7; 34:19; Hebrews 2:14-15)

- **Provider** – He loves to provide for His children's every need, and He is so faithful in doing so. (Psalm 34:9-10; 36:8-9; 84:11; Matthew 6:31-33)

You simply cannot get a better character than the character of God Himself!

Intrinsic Value

If the Intrinsic value of just one of us is worth more than the combined wealth of the planet, how on earth could we estimate the Intrinsic value of Almighty God? It is truly OFF THE CHARTS!!!

Can you imagine what would happen in our communities if this God fully lived and walked amongst us and was free to manifest the fulness of who He is in whatever way He desired to do? That's what He's wanting to do.

God's Original Plan
I Want to Be Me

It has always been the cry on the heart of God to have a people who will value Him for who He is, express His worth appropriately, and allow Him to be all that He is to them. I was stunned to find in Genesis what the core essence of the covenant that God made with Abraham was. In Genesis 17:7 it says, *"I will establish My covenant between Me and you and your descendants after you throughout their generations for an everlasting covenant, **to be God to you** and to your descendants after you."* God was saying, "I want to be Me! Will you let Me be Me to you?" He was wanting us to live in such a relationship of honor with Him, recognizing His worth and value, and expressing that to Him, that He could be free to be Himself to us.

Time and time again in Scripture we find God expressing the longing of His heart. Look at the following examples:

> "'Moreover, I will make My dwelling among you, and My soul will not reject you. I will also walk among you and be your God, and you shall be My people.'" —Leviticus 26:11-12

> "'I will give them a heart to know Me, for I am the Lord; and they will be My people, and I will be their God, for they will

return to Me with their whole heart.'" —Jeremiah 24:7

"And I will give them one heart, and put a new spirit within them. And I will take the heart of stone out of their flesh and give them a heart of flesh, that they may walk in My statutes and keep My ordinances and do them. Then they will be My people, and I shall be their God." —Ezekiel 11:19-20

ISRAEL, GOD'S EXAMPLE TO THE NATIONS

God's plan was to take one ethnic group, the Hebrews, and live amongst them with such freedom to be Himself that other nations would look on and see a living example of what a nation looked like when God was living with them – in freedom, wisdom, prosperity, protection, abundance, generosity, joy, peace – and that it would arouse desire within them for Him, and cause them to say, "We want in on this! We want the life and liberty you have!"

"And I will make you a great nation, and I will bless you, and make your name great; and so you shall be a blessing; and I will bless those who bless you, and the one who curses you I will curse. And in you all the families of the earth will be blessed." —Genesis 12:2-3

THE PRIESTHOOD

He invited the whole nation to be priests before Him – *"'Now then, if you will indeed obey My voice and keep My covenant, then you shall be My own possession among all the peoples, for all the earth is Mine; and you shall be to Me a kingdom of priests and a holy nation.' These are the words that you shall speak to the sons of Israel." (Exodus 19:5-6)* But they turned the invitation down and asked Moses to be the one who would interact with God instead of them. So God, in effect, said, "Alright, if I can't have a nation,

I'll have a tribe," and He chose the tribe of Levi to recognize His worth and value, and to express that to Him appropriately and consistently.

If we track Israel's history in the Old Testament, we will see a distinct up-and-down graph line. At one stage, the nation would be at peace, secure from its enemies, in prosperity, and worshiping God with sincerity. Then would commence a period of decline where they lost their relationship with God, they became vulnerable to their enemies – were raided and harassed by them, they lost their prosperity, and then they would hit rock bottom. They were put under real pressure by the neighboring nations, endured lots of wars and, in some cases, were invaded and taken as captives. After a period of time they would recognize how far away from their relationship with God and their destiny they had fallen; after they cried out for a deliverer, God would listen to their pleas and rescue them. They would re-establish their relationship with God, He would deal with their enemies, and they would start again, back at the place of prominence and influence, prosperity and peace. This cycle repeated itself many times in their history, and with each cycle it would be with a new generation of people. One of the major causes for the decline, however, was exactly the same with each generation – the priesthood chose to dishonor God.

The Value Statement – an expression of Honor

If you and I were alive during that period of Old Testament history, we would be very familiar with a protocol that was part of the culture of that time. If we wanted to go into the presence of a king, a dignitary or a high-ranking official, we would never go empty-handed. We would take with us a gift which was a "value statement" – it expressed the value we placed on the person we were meeting with. It was, in effect, a statement to the person, saying, "This is what I think of you."

Many of the Old Covenant sacrifices had the same symbolism in the context of the nation's relationship to God – they were value statements, indicating the value that the people placed on God. One of the requirements that God made of the priesthood was that the offering should be "the best."

> "'But if his offering for a sacrifice of peace offerings to the Lord is from the flock, he shall offer it, male or female, without defect.'" —Leviticus 3:6

Why did God want the best? Was that selfish of Him, always wanting the best for Himself? Not at all. **The only appropriate value statement that could be given to God was "the best" because God is the best!**

As the priesthood lived and carried out their ministry in a way that expressed the awesome value of who God is, He was free to be Himself among them. What eventually happened, however, was that the priesthood lost sight of the value and worth of God, and instead of offering Him the best in their sacrifices, they would find an animal that was diseased or crippled and offer Him that. In effect, they were saying to themselves, "This animal's no good to me any more because of its sickness, so I'll give it to God." In doing so they were saying to God, "This is what I think of You!"

Remember what we looked at in chapter 3 – *When you dishonor a person, you shut yourself off from receiving who they are and what they have to give.* Israel was shutting themselves off from being able to receive who God was, and who He wanted to be to them, so that put a huge limit on what He could do for them and be to them without violating the principles of relationship that He had already established.

God picks up on this lack of honor from the priesthood in Malachi.

> "A son honors his father, and a slave his master. If I am a father, where is the honor due me? If I am a master, where is the respect due me?" says the LORD Almighty. It is you priests who show contempt for my name. But you ask, 'How have we shown contempt for your name?' By offering defiled food on my altar. But you ask, 'How have we defiled you?' By saying that the LORD's table is contemptible. When you offer blind animals for sacrifice, is that not wrong? When you sacrifice lame or diseased animals, is that not wrong? Try offering them to your governor! Would he be pleased with you? Would he accept you?" says the LORD Almighty.
> —Malachi 1:6-8 (NIV)

The Power of the Priesthood

We have already seen that God made a covenant with Abraham to bless every nation through His relationship with the nation of Israel. Later in Israel's history, God also made a covenant with David concerning his throne and the Levitical Priesthood.

> "For thus says the LORD, 'David shall never lack a man to sit on the throne of the house of Israel; and **the Levitical priests shall never lack a man before Me to offer burnt offerings, to burn grain offerings and to prepare sacrifices continually.'"** The word of the LORD came to Jeremiah, saying, "Thus says the LORD, 'If you can break My covenant for the day and My covenant for the night, so that day and night will not be at their appointed time, then My covenant may also be broken with David My servant so that he will not have a son to reign on his throne, **and with the Levitical priests, My ministers."**
> —Jeremiah 33:17-21

In that covenant, God established the permanency of the throne of David. Jesus, David's descendant, was the fulfillment of that promise – Jesus' reign will never end. But God also promised that He would always have a priesthood who would offer sacrifices and minister to Him. Did the Levitical priesthood continue forever? No, it didn't, because the Levitical priesthood finished at the cross, but the priesthood did continue after the cross as the New Covenant priesthood.

> You also, as living stones, are being built up as a spiritual house for a holy priesthood, to offer up spiritual sacrifices acceptable to God through Jesus Christ. —1 Peter 2:5

> But you are A CHOSEN RACE, A royal PRIESTHOOD, A HOLY NATION, A PEOPLE FOR God's OWN POSSESSION, so that you may proclaim the excellencies of Him who has called you out of darkness into His marvelous light. —1 Peter 2:9

If you are in relationship with Jesus, if you have been born again, you are a New Covenant priest with the right and responsibility to offer sacrifices to God (spiritual sacrifices, not animal sacrifices), to minister to Him, and to proclaim the wonder of who He is – to make accurately known His identity and His worth. What a privilege!

We asked earlier, how would the enemy try and prevent this relationship between God and His people from really flourishing? One of the ways he can do this is by getting the people of God to operate in dishonor towards God. It is exactly the same strategy that he used with the Old Covenant priesthood. When the priesthood functions in dishonor towards God, then He can't be who He is to them, and to the people that the priesthood represents.

ooOoo

REFLECTION POINTS

- Consider the following statement – *"When you recognize and value God for 'who He is,' and express that appropriately to Him, it causes a response in Him ... it releases Him to be 'who He is' to you!"* What are some ways that the truth of that statement could impact your life?

- When you look at God's record of Performance, how does that affect your ability and willingness to trust Him for every situation you face?

- Think about the various aspects of God's Position as listed in the section "Value due to Position" – Creator, Source, Owner, etc. In which of those aspects have you seen Him function in your life? What did that look like, and how did it affect you?

- What aspects of His Character have you come to experience so far? What did that look like, and how did it affect you? What aspects of His Character have you yet to experience? Ask Him to lead you in experience of those aspects of who He is.

Chapter 6

THE MOST SIGNIFICANT RELATIONSHIP OF ALL

WHAT SATAN FEARS MOST

Many people think that there is a titanic struggle in the universe between the forces of darkness and the Kingdom of Light, between God and Satan. That couldn't be further from the truth! For Satan to pick a fight with God is about the same as an ant picking a fight with an elephant. It's not even fair! Satan is a created being who does have a realm of authority in which to operate, but it is limited in both time and scope. He is a defeated foe who has been disarmed at Calvary, and the only power that he has over us, if we are in relationship with Jesus, is the power that we will allow him to have.

There is one thing that I believe Satan fears more than anything else – for God to show up and be Himself; for Him to show up and display the wonder of who He really is! Satan does not have the judicial authority to overturn anything that God wants to do, but he does understand the power of honor, and the principle of relationship that God has established in the earth, and he knows how to use it to his advantage. **The relationship that he fears most is the relationship between God and His people**, and if he can be instrumental in getting the people of God to operate in dishonor, he need not worry about God showing up and being Himself.

> Jesus said to them, "A prophet is not without honor except in his hometown and among his own relatives and in his own household." And He could do no miracle there except that He laid His hands on a few sick people and healed them.
> —Mark 6:4-5

Dishonor restricted Jesus and held Him back from being who He was to the people in His own hometown.

We see a similar response in the gospel of John.

> The Jews answered and said to Him, "Do we not say rightly that You are a Samaritan and have a demon?" Jesus answered, "I do not have a demon; but I honor My Father, and you dishonor Me."
> —John 8:48-49

The single most significant relationship in the universe is the relationship between God and His people.

If God really shows up and expresses the wonder of who He is, and if the people of God understand who they really are and live out of that identity, then Satan's kingdom will be in ruins. I believe we will see unprecedented demonstrations of the love and power of God, and there will be a viral outbreak of sonship and a supernatural expansion of the Kingdom in the earth! The people of the earth will finally see an accurate expression of who God really is, and will understand and experience the truth that they are genuinely loved and celebrated – by God and by His family. Countless millions will be swept into the Kingdom in the greatest ingathering of souls that the world has ever seen!

The enemy has no countermeasure at his disposal if that happens. His only strategy is to try and stop it from happening in the first place. How?

Let's review some of what we've learned so far.

God has created the world to function in the context of relationship, and He knows that no relationship can blossom and grow unless each person in that relationship recognizes the value in the other and expresses that, appropriately and consistently.

God is doing His part in the relationship. He has crowned us with glory and honor, He has glorified us – *clothed us with splendor, rendered us excellent, caused our dignity and worth to become manifest and acknowledged* – He is continually expressing His delight in us, and honoring us, in so many ways. The One who created us to ask those two questions, "Who am I?" and "What am I worth?" is Himself asking those two questions of us – "Who am I?" and "What am I worth?" – and the whole spirit realm is poised, waiting with baited breath for the answer, because our response will determine, in large measure, how much God can be Himself amongst us.

The New Covenant Priesthood

So how does this work in our relationship with God as New Covenant priests?

We saw in a previous chapter that every offering is, in fact, a value statement – it says, "This is what I think of you." We also saw that in expressing honor, it wasn't enough to use just words, but that our attitudes, responses and actions were equally involved – it is a "whole being" expression.

We know that Jesus, when talking to the woman at the well, cut right through the peripheral issues that she was focusing on and spoke to her about the heart of worship. He said in John 4:23-24: *"But an hour is coming, and now is, when the true worshipers will worship the Father in spirit and truth; for such people the Father seeks to be His worshipers. God is spirit, and those who worship Him must worship in spirit and truth."*

He used the phrase "true worshipers," implying there were false worshipers ... that there is a form of worship that is not actually genuine, not the real deal. It looks like the real thing, but it is not. Jesus then went on to explain what, from God's perspective, is real, genuine worship. He said that it must be "in spirit" and "in truth." I would have loved it if He had amplified that a bit, if He had given us more information on what that really looked like, but He didn't.

SPIRIT TO SPIRIT

In essence, this is what I believe He meant. God is essentially a spirit being, and we are made in His image. We, also, are essentially spirit beings. We have a soul and we live in a body, but the real essential *us* is spirit. *God set the world up to function in the context of relationship, and He knew that another component needed for any relationship to grow and be healthy was that the two people in that relationship must connect spirit to spirit.*

Have you ever been talking to another person and you can just tell that they are not really interested in what you are saying? They may be nodding at appropriate moments, but their body language tells you that their attention is really somewhere else, their eyes are roaming round the room and not even looking at you. It doesn't feel good, does it? But you could be talking to another person and they're looking right at you, making all the right responses at the right times, and still you feel that you're not really important to them, that they're not really engaged with what you're saying. Now, how would you know that? I mean, their body language is doing all the right things, but somehow that isn't enough. It's a hard thing to quantify, but you actually pick that up in your spirit!

You can tell, when you're talking to another person, when you feel that you're really connecting. You feel really great, you feel that you're important to them, that you have value and that you're worth listening to. You may not be analyzing what's happening, but the truth is, you are connecting with that person, spirit to spirit. When that happens there is a flow of life between you and the other person.

If *you* can tell whether you are connecting with another person or not, don't you think that God, who is the ultimate spirit person, can tell when we are just being polite to Him, or when our spirit is engaged and we are really communicating with Him? Listen to the heart of God expressed in Isaiah 29:13: *"The Lord says: 'These people come near to me with their mouth and honor me with their lips, but their hearts are far from me. Their worship of me is based on merely human rules they have been taught.'"* (NIV)

A New Covenant Spiritual Sacrifice

Let's consider a very common experience for many in the Body of Christ – a weekly church service.

I want to present to you a hypothetical scenario that is very realistic. In this scenario is a man whom we'll call Barry. Barry is a Christian, a young married man with two children, who works a 40-hour week in an office. In the last week he has been hassled by his boss in an unfair manner, he has some major bills that have yet to be paid, and his kids have been squabbling more than usual, creating quite a bit of tension in the home. He had a staff party last night, which was really good but did finish late, so now on Sunday morning he's off to church feeling really tired and very focused on the problems of the week. The worship team starts worshiping, and Barry joins in, kind of enjoying the beat of the songs but, apart from that, with nothing else really happening for him. There's nothing really coming from his spirit, no engaging with God, no borrowing the words of the songwriter to express something that he wants to say to God. He's just doing what he usually does on Sundays – sings the songs.

Barry may have been singing words that express the greatness of God, or how much he loves God, but through his attitudes and responses this is what Barry has been saying to God nonverbally: *"God, I completely ignore Your value due to Performance (the wonder of what You've done), I ignore and discount Your value due to Position (Your incredible greatness), I ignore Your value due to Character (the wonder of who You are) and I have no regard for Your Intrinsic value. What is far more important to me is what I'm feeling and what I'm going through right now."* By withholding any expression from his spirit of the worth of God, as a New Covenant priest he has just given God the equivalent of a blind, diseased Old Covenant sacrifice; he has just given God "any old thing" and said to God, "This is what I think of You."

Do you realize that most of our value statements to God are nonverbal? They are most often communicated in our attitudes, responses and actions.

The Manifest Presence of God

Why is it that, in so many of our churches across the globe, we experience so little of the manifest presence of God? There may be many factors that contribute to the answer to that question, but I believe we must consider this: Have we, as the people of God, as New Covenant priests, been giving God "any old thing" as an expression of His worth?

Is there power in praise and worship? Absolutely! But where does that power reside? Does it reside in the fact that the people of God come together and sing the right words? No! We have already established – the words alone will not cut it! The power of praise and worship is released when the group of people who have gathered express the wonder of who God is in worship, AND their attitudes, responses, and actions during the week are saying the same thing! It is a whole being expression. When we stand before Him, in spite of difficult circumstances, feelings of weariness, and any other negative things that we contend with, we can acknowledge how we feel but then we focus on the wonder of who He is and what He's done! As we declare that to Him with our whole hearts, and we expect to encounter Him, you can be certain that He knows that He is welcome.

ooOoo

Reflection Points

- Think about the following statement made in relation to Satan: *"...the only power that he has over us, if we are in relationship with Jesus, is the power that we will allow him to have."* In what ways do we allow him to have power over us?

- Can you remember times when you really connected with another person, spirit to spirit? How did that make you feel?

- Think of the times when you really connected with God, spirit to Spirit. What happened, and how did that affect you?

- Consider the scenario with Barry in this chapter. Can you identify in your own life any of the negative non-verbal value statements that he made to God by his attitudes and responses? If so, what things could you do that would change that pattern of response?

- What would be some practical ways that you could give God "your best" as a statement of His worth to you, instead of giving Him "any old thing"?

Chapter 7

WILL SOMEBODY LET ME BE ME!

God is consistently saying to His church, "Will somebody let Me be Me!"

I remember an incident many years ago when God first confronted my attitude towards Him. I was resisting Him and I had no idea that I was doing it. I grew up in a home where classical music was constantly played, and if I wanted to relax that would be my "go to" place; my preference in style of music – even many years later. Coupled with this was an assumption that I had made in regard to sung worship, and I really have no idea where I picked it up from. The assumption was this - *the only style of worship that God would accept, that He really loved, was the softer worship songs that expressed love to Him.* I found that when I was in worship times where the music and lyrical content got stronger, louder and more militant, with a more driving beat, I would get agitated and inside I would begin to shut down. I felt very uncomfortable and wanted the atmosphere to get back to some *real* worship. What I didn't realize was that I had locked God into the box of *my personal preference.* I assumed that because I liked a particular style of worship, of course, that was the style of worship that God would like! When the worship atmosphere was different from how I liked it – what I thought pleased God – I resisted it and judged it.

One Sunday night, I was ministering at a church in the Gold Coast of Australia, where I was to speak on the topic of worship. Leading the worship time in that service was a Christian band called "Sons of Thunder." They had just released an album called "Angry Young Men" because they were angry at the devil, so before the service began I was at the back of the church praying up a storm, thinking, "Oh, no! How am I going to turn this service around and get it going where I need it to go?" Then it came time to begin the service; the band started up, and did they go for it! It was high volume, but the songs were faith-inspiring, their hearts were in love with Jesus, and an atmosphere of the presence of God filled the room. By the third or fourth song, I was lifted into a realm of God's anointing that I had not experienced before. When it came time for me to speak, I preached with freedom and passion, and when I gave a response time at the end for those who wanted a fresh touch from the Lord, the band came back on stage and played exactly what was needed for that atmosphere.

On that night God did something to my prejudices and lack of understanding – He blew them to bits! He said to me, *"Rob, when it comes to relating to Me, your personal preferences in styles of music and worship are totally irrelevant. I am way bigger than you will ever know, and there is much more to who I am than you have currently experienced."* He showed me how I had locked Him into the box of my personal preference, and that He had absolutely no intention of being bound by it. He said, "How can two walk together unless they are in agreement," and then He told me, "I am the God who doesn't change, so guess who's going to have to change!" I didn't like it at the time, but something definitely stirred within me in the weeks that followed – a real sense of excitement that there was more for me to discover about Him.

A MULTI-FACETED BEING, A MULTI-FACETED RELATIONSHIP

This is what He showed me: There are many parallels between a relationship with God and a relationship with other people, but there are some differences as well. One of the reasons for the differences is because in relating to God we are dealing with an infinite being – there are so many facets to who He is. Because of this, He has given us different cameos in Scripture; different pictures that describe aspects of who He is.

Some examples:

Father/Child

God is the Father and we are His children.

Many times God wants to relate to us as our Father – for us to know the love and security of snuggling into Daddy's arms – of knowing the certainty of His provision for us and protection of us. Other times He has to bring loving but firm correction or instruction to us, all for our benefit. (Psalm 103:13-14; Matthew 6:30-34)

King/Subject

Jesus Christ is our King and we are His subjects.

There are times when the Holy Spirit will want to direct our attention to the majestic splendor of the King of kings, to proclaim His Kingship and His supreme reign over our lives and over all the earth. In a meeting there can come a sense of participating in a regal procession with fanfare, pomp, ceremony, celebration etc., crowning Him as Lord of lords! At the same time we are automatically declaring our submission to His Kingship and that His Word is law in our lives! (Deuteronomy 10:17; Psalm 24:7-10; Psalm 145:10-13; 1 Timothy 6:14-16; Romans 8:7; Luke 6:46)

Creator/Created

God is the Creator and we are His creation.

There will be times when the Holy Spirit will want to direct our attention to His creative genius as seen in the wonder, intricacy, and variety of His creation; to marvel at His handiwork and appreciate Him for it. (Job 38-39; Psalms 8:3-4; 19:1-4; 92:4; 104:24,33-34; 111:2; 143:5-6; Isaiah 40:21-28)

Bridegroom/Bride

Jesus Christ is the Bridegroom and we are His bride.

From this mode of relating comes the love songs in worship, the ability to express our deep love for Him and to receive His expressions of love for us. (Isaiah 62:5; 2 Corinthians 11:2; Ephesians 3:17-19)

Commander/Army

God is the commander of the armies of heaven and we are His army.

There will be times when the Lord will direct us to rise up in our spirits and be militant in our declaration of authority over the powers of darkness. He expects us to be able to respond as one man – a disciplined unit of believers who are obedient to His commands! (Psalm 24:8; 1 Timothy 1:18; 2 Timothy 2:4; Ephesians 6:12; Revelation 19:11-16)

Regarding these last two, this was my dilemma – I had assumed that the only appropriate way to relate to God was in the Bride/Bridegroom mode and, besides, that was my personal preference. So He had to say to me, "Are you free to relate to Me as the Commander when I'm wanting to relate to you in that way?" I had to confess that I wasn't free to relate to Him as Commander – it felt uncomfortable and was certainly outside the box of my personal preference musically! Since that time He's taken me on an amazing adventure of discovery in my relationship with Him, and I'm way freer to engage with Him in a more militant way than I used to be. The styles of music and worship that I enjoy have increased hugely, but I'm still learning and He's still stretching me.

Some people will only relate to God as Bride/Bridegroom, but there are definitely times when God wants to relate to us as the Commander of His army. What do you think it would be like if a soldier in the army came up to his general and said, "General … Oh, how I love you!" He'd get a few days of double duties, at least! And yet that happens so many times in our church gatherings, when God is wanting to relate to us in a more militant way and His people are still saying, "I love You." It's like He needs to say, "It's not time for that now."

There are more…

Holy God/Priest

God is Holy and we are His priests.

We are called to minister to Him and bring to Him acceptable sacrifices that will please Him. The Holy Spirit often brings such an awareness of the holiness of God and the very real sense that we are standing on holy ground! Sometimes the only appropriate response is stillness and silence in His presence! (Hebrews 13:15; 1 Peter 2:5)

Shepherd/Sheep

The Lord is our shepherd and we are His sheep.

Often He will want to lead us by still waters, cause us to lie down in green pastures, and restore our souls in His presence – the beautiful, gentle ministry of the shepherd who cares for the needs of his flock in provision and healing! (Psalm 23:1-3; Isaiah 40:11; Ezekiel 34:11-12,15-16) Also in this aspect of His nature comes the guiding presence and ability of the shepherd to help us stay on track and get us where we need to go.

These different aspects of who He is can be engaged with, both in our individual times with Him and in our corporate times as a church family.

God knows when we are having difficulty relating to Him in various ways, but He wants us to grow in our ability to relate to Him. Many of us have difficulty relating to God as Father because of difficulties in our relationship with our earthly father. Some of us prefer relating to the Lord as the Bridegroom rather than as the Commander. Some of us prefer to focus on the gentle healing ministry of the Lord as our Shepherd.

God is calling us to fullness of maturity in these days, and He wants us to be able to freely respond to Him in any and all of these ways, at any given time or place. We need to understand two very important things:

1) God accepts us totally as we are (John 6:37), and

2) He has absolutely no intention that we stay as we are! (Romans 8:29)

God wants to deal with every hindrance in our relationship with Him so that we can be free to respond to Him as He intends us to. *"...the Lord is the Spirit, and where the Spirit of the Lord is, there is freedom." (2 Corinthians 3:17 NIV)*

So how is it in your local church, and in your times with Him individually?

Are there times when...

- You experience the manifest love of the Father in your personal and corporate times, as He gathers you to His heart?
- You are caught up with the wonder of His regal splendor, with the presence of the King of Kings in your midst and the knowledge that all things are under His control?
- You are caught up in the wonder of what He has made, where you "sing for joy at the work of His hands," where you appreciate Him for His creative genius?
- You are captivated by His love for you and you express your love for Him, experiencing the intimacy of shared affection?
- You sense His call to stand and militantly declare the truth of His Word and the unshakeable nature of His character, and you respond as one man, in unity and cohesion?
- You are caught up in wonder as you worship at His Throne, the sense of His majesty and holiness fills the atmosphere, and a holy hush descends on you as you wait in His presence?
- You sense Jesus calling you to come to Him and let Him minister to you His healing, refreshing of your soul, leading you beside still waters?

...or are some of those experiences missing?

If He wants us to honor Him with wild celebration and dancing, are we free to respond to Him in that way, or do we say, "I'm sorry, but I don't do that," or "We don't do that in our church!"

If He wants us to give a militant shout of authority against the demonic realm that is trying to bring us into bondage, are we free to respond in obedience to Him, or do we say, "I'm sorry, but I'm just not comfortable with that!"

Manifestations of His Glory

For hundreds of years the church has been praying, "*Your Kingdom come, Your will be done, on earth as it is in heaven.*" We have been asking for the realm of heaven to be manifest in the earth, but most of us have no idea what we've been asking for! In recent years there has been a huge increase of manifestations of the glory of God around the globe. These manifestations include:

- Oil appearing supernaturally – on people's hands, on their Bible, from the pulpit, down the walls
- Gold dust or sapphire dust appearing supernaturally
- Gemstones appearing supernaturally
- Feathers appearing supernaturally
- A glory cloud appearing in midair
- Fire appearing on people's heads or over a church building
- Angels being seen
- Angelic choirs singing
- Angels supernaturally playing instruments after the musicians have stopped playing
- Jesus appearing to people and revealing who He really is. In many cases it is to people who do not even believe in Him.

- People being instantly transported from one location in the earth to another location, often hundreds of miles away.

Many Christians have become really offended with God when they hear of these things happening. They often say, "Why would God do that!?" I love what Joshua Mills says – "If you've got a problem with a feather, you're sure going to have a problem with a whole angel!" We've been asking for the heavenly realm to manifest in the earth, yet when it does we say, "Oh, I didn't mean like that!!" Come on, people, we might just have some growing up to do. I believe that we are moving towards a time where we will see unprecedented miracles and demonstrations of the love and power of God in the earth. *Unprecedented* means "never seen before." Everything in the list above has already been seen in the earth, so what does God have in store for a people who really want Him to show up and be Himself? What will *"unprecedented"* look like? I wonder!

God is saying, "Will you let Me be Me!" and around the globe there are people who are hearing His heart cry and responding with hunger and passion. They want to have God back in His church!

Is He the Head of the Church?

We saw in chapter 5, when looking at who He is, that He is the Head of the Church. That may be easy for us to say, or to sing about, but is He? In my local church? Really? I hope so, but I've been on pastoral staff in various churches for over 40 years and I know something of the challenges that we can face in church life.

How easy it is for us to say, "Lord, this is Your church," and then by our attitudes, responses, and actions, we tell Him what He can and cannot do in our services and in what time frame He can do it.

What are some practical implications, if it really is God's church and not ours?

- We will be asking, "God, what do you want us to be doing in our community? How do You want us to represent You here?"
- We will be asking, "God, what are You wanting to happen in this service?"
- We will prioritize the presence of God and we will prioritize His agenda for our times together, as much as we are able to sense that.
- If God is wanting to reveal some aspect of His nature and character to us, we will respond to Him and engage with Him in the way that He is choosing to relate to us.
- If the worship needs to go longer than usual, we will run with that and either extend the time of our meeting or reduce the time of the message.
- If His priority in a given meeting is what He wants to say to us in the preaching of the Word, we can condense the sung worship component of our time together and make room for the teaching.

The Relationship of Honor in Daily Life

The relationship of honor isn't just relevant to church worship times; it relates to every area of our lives.

Let's suppose that the Holy Spirit prompts me to give a particular person $1,000. I have a variety of responses available to me on receiving such a prompting, one of which is, "How much??!!" Then this thought comes into my head, "Well, it's Your money so You can do what you like with it." And I come into agreement with that thought. But then I have another thought, "If I give $1,000, then that's $1,000 less that I'll have in my bank account, and I'll have to work some overtime to make up the difference, because it's my responsibility to provide for myself." And I come into agreement with that thought. Do you know what's just happened? Without saying a single word, I have just told God by my response and my attitude, "You are not the owner of all things. This is my money and I can do with it what I like." I've just told Him, "You are not my provider. It is my responsibility to provide for myself." Guess what He can't be to me now, in the way that He wants to, in the context of our relationship? He can't be the One with authority over my possessions, and He can't be the Provider that He wants to be to me, because I've just told Him that He isn't those things. The very thing that I need Him to be to me, my Provider, I've now blocked and made a lot more difficult because of my dishonor of Him.

But I didn't have to choose those responses in that situation. I could have said, "Wow, Lord, I sure wasn't expecting that instruction, but this is Your money, and I'm a steward of it, so if You say to give $1,000 to that person, then I give it willingly. And Lord, as I sow this money into that person's life, I look to You for the harvest and increase from the seed I've sown, and I thank You for it in advance because You are my Provider and You are totally faithful to meet all my needs!" And God is saying, "Atta boy! You are affirming to Me that I am the Owner of your possessions and I am Your Provider, so I am free to be that to you!"

What are some other ways we can express honor to God?

- Acknowledge His presence in every situation. If you are present in a group of people where none of them acknowledge your presence in any way, and no one talks to you, it's not a nice feeling. God is no different. He loves it when we acknowledge that He is with us in the office, in the classroom, in the factory, when we're having recreation time, and when we include Him in our thoughts and internal conversation.

- Reprioritize our schedule on occasion, so we replace doing something else with having special time with Him. That communicates to Him that we place greater value on our time with Him than on the thing we would have previously been doing.
- Give the first fruits of our finance to Him, acknowledging Him as our Source and our Provider.
- Choose to trust Him in all circumstances, especially the ones where we don't understand or see what He is up to.
- Thank Him for what He's doing in our circumstances.

The Power of Thanksgiving

This brings up another really important principle outlined in Scripture – the power of thanksgiving.

In the Old Testament, one of the words which we translate into the English language as "thanksgiving" or "thank offering" is the Hebrew word *Todah*, which has three primary shades of meaning:

- To make a vow
- To lift the hands in adoration
- To give thanks – some Lexicons mention that this has a particular emphasis of *giving thanks for things not yet received.*

Psalm 50:23 says, *"He who offers a sacrifice of thanksgiving [Todah] honors Me;"* and the next part of the verse is rendered differently by different versions. NASB reads, *"And to him who orders his way aright I shall show the salvation of God."* Another version reads, *"And prepares the way so that I may show him the salvation of God."* I like the sense of what this is saying. *"He who offers a sacrifice of thanksgiving honors me, and prepares the way so that I may show him the salvation of God."*

When we are in a difficult situation, the instinctive, natural response can be to complain and become negative and cynical. What God is saying is that in the midst of difficulty, when we choose to lift our hands in adoration, and thank Him in advance for what He is going to do, we honor Him – we recognize His identity and worth, we refuse to be swayed by the appearance of our circumstances – and by our response we literally prepare a way in the spirit realm for Him to get to us the very thing that we've been believing for. The power of laying hold of who God is through thanksgiving breaks through every demonic stronghold of oppression and resistance and clears the way for the angelic hosts to bring the answer to our prayers. That is incredibly powerful!

A number of years ago we were in a situation where we were struggling financially. The unpaid bills were piling up and it seemed like our prayers to the Lord for provision were going completely unanswered. Lyn had paintings that were for sale, but they had not sold. I was teaching music full time during that year, but then a number of the students I gave lessons to moved out of district, so my income from teaching was down. Besides, our son Dan had recently moved to Auckland with us and had been looking for a job, but hadn't found anything. Circumstantially, it was not looking good. Emotionally, I was not feeling good. I was out in my study one morning, feeling pretty low, and during my prayer time, I was having a good old complain to God. I felt really justified in doing so, too, because He just wasn't coming through with what He had promised. Right in the middle of my complaining, the Lord spoke clearly to my spirit and He said, "Rob, quit the complaining – sing to your circumstances!" That was NOT what I wanted to hear. I knew exactly what He was saying, because I understood the principle of giving thanks for things not yet received, but it was not what I was walking in right at that moment. How easily we can understand the right thing to do but still not choose to do it.

I had a very important decision to make. Everything within me wanted to continue in my preoccupation with self-pity and complaint, but I also knew that to stay on that course of action would only lead to a downward spiral of negative attitudes and emotions. So without feeling the least bit spiritual, I chose to obey what the Lord had told me to do. He could have said, "Speak to your circumstances," and that would have been equally valid, but in this case He said, "Sing to your circumstances." So I just began to make up a spontaneous tune and began to sing words like, "Father, I thank You that You are our provider and that You will not fail us. I thank You for Lyn's paintings selling, and I decree favor over them right now in Your Name. I thank You, Lord, for new music students, and I call them in, in Jesus' Name. I thank You for the job that You have for Dan, and that it will be the best job for him, totally suited to who he is and the skill set that he has." When I started singing, I felt nothing emotionally or spiritually, but as I kept making those decrees and giving thanks, something began to change in my heart, and I began to dance around the room and celebrate Him and His goodness.

Nothing changed that day, or the day after that, but within a few days, Lyn's paintings began to sell and I began to get phone calls from people who asked, "Do you teach music?" and more music students began to come in. Within two weeks, all Lyn's paintings had sold and Dan got a job doing computer animation and 3D graphics for a company that he is still with to this day. I am convinced that my decision that day to obey God and release thanksgiving to Him, regardless of what I was seeing around me circumstantially, cleared a way in the spirit realm for Him to bring me the very things that I had been asking Him for.

ATTACK ON IDENTITY

We need to understand that the majority of the attacks of the enemy that we will face in this life are related to the issue of identity – God's and ours. Our relationship with God will automatically flow from our understanding of who He is. If you think that God is a strict judge whose primary focus is your Performance and on you getting everything right, and whose judgment will fall on you when you do something wrong, you will relate to Him on that basis. Your life will be filled with rules and regulations, and you will be hard on yourself and on others because you have to be right and do things right. If the enemy can distort your perception of God, he will do so, because he knows how it will turn your relationship with God septic.

What was the first thing that Jesus heard from the Father at the beginning of His ministry? An affirmation of His identity:

"You are my beloved son, in whom I am well pleased!" (Mark 1:11 WEB) What was the first thing that Satan attacked when testing Jesus? His identity. *"If you are the Son of God..."* (Matthew 4:3)

When you or I make a declaration as to the identity and worth of God, whether it be spoken or sung in worship, don't ever assume that Satan's response to that will be, "Dang it! I was hoping that they wouldn't find that out!" At the outset, our declarations of God's worth and identity are no threat to Satan whatsoever. His initial response to any such declaration is always, "Really? We'll see about that!" Our declaration will always be challenged by the enemy. It's what happens next that has the potential to be the major threat to the enemy.

When we are confronted with a difficult situation that we don't know how to resolve, we have basically two options:

1. Worry, which means that we have taken control and have said nonverbally to God, "You aren't big enough to handle this one, so I've got to sort this out myself," or
2. Take it to God, thank Him in advance for what He's going to do on your behalf in this situation, and look for His solution and His resources.

You may have sung all the songs you like about God reigning and His faithfulness, but when the enemy confronts you with the difficulty of a situation and the meagerness of your resources to handle it, saying, "Oh yeah, is God really able to handle this?" he is challenging your earlier declaration. He is challenging the identity and character of God. It's only when you continue to affirm that earlier declaration and, by your response and attitude, affirm your trust in Him and your praise of Him, that you will absolutely win out over the enemy and his strategy to sabotage the power of your relationship with God.

ooOoo

Reflection Points

- Which of the following aspects of who God is – Father, King, Creator, Bridegroom, Commander, Holy God, Shepherd

–do you find it easiest to relate to Him as? Which aspects of who He is do you find the most difficult to relate to? Why do you think that is? What are some practical steps that you can take to help you grow in your ability to relate to Him in these different ways?

- Are there any expressions of worship that you are internally resistant to (e.g., lifting your hands, clapping, bowing, dancing, wild celebration, shouting, militant declaration, procession, kneeling, prostrating yourself, silence)? What do you think is the cause of that resistance?

- What supernatural manifestations of God's glory have you experienced so far? What happened, and how did that make you feel?

- If you are a leader in a local church, what challenges do you face in sensing God's agenda for a given meeting, and making room for that? How have you overcome those challenges?

- Many of our attitudes and responses in daily life communicate to God what we think of Him. Having learned that, how do you think that will affect your relationship with Him?

- Can you think of any situations you have faced where you have deliberately thanked God ahead of time for the answer that you were believing for? If so, how did that affect you, and how did it affect your circumstances?

- In what situations have you experienced the enemy attacking your sense of identity, or challenging who you have already declared God to be? What was your response to that, and what happened as a result?

Chapter 8

WHAT THE WORLD NEEDS NOW

A number of years ago, Burt Bacharach wrote a song titled "What the world needs now," which circled the globe and became an international hit. It contained the following lyrics, *"What the world needs now is love, sweet love. It's the only thing that there's just too little of..."* That statement is undoubtedly true, but I believe there is an even greater thing that the world needs, which will release the "love, sweet love" that Burt Bacharach wrote about.

What the world needs now is for the most significant relationship in the universe, the relationship between God and His people, to come into its fullness of maturity so that each party in that relationship can be who they really are! *The world needs God to be who He really is,* and *the world needs you and me to be who we really are.*

For years the cry of my heart, and that of many others in the Body of Christ, has been, "God, we just need You to move in our church. We need a mighty move of Your Spirit in our nation!" So many of us have cried out to God for revival, and I believe that those prayers have definitely been heard. But recently the Lord began to show me that when we pray like that, we are only seeing half the picture.

The Anatomy of a Lightning Strike

He said to me, "I want you to learn about lightning strikes." I was somewhat surprised by this, but I began to look on the Internet for information on lightning, and I came across an amazing video clip on YouTube.[4] This clip tells of some research done by Dr. Geoff McHarg at the U.S. Air Force Atmospheric Research Centre in Colorado Springs. He uses a very high speed video camera and manages to capture the birth of a lightning bolt as it descends from the clouds to the earth, and then he slows the camera down over 200 times slower as it replays the action so we can see exactly what happens.

A flash of light darts out of the cloud and zigzags downward in roughly 50-yard segments. This first stage of lightning is called a "stepped leader." It is looking for ground, going back and forth. As this stepped leader gets close to the earth, it has an extraordinary effect on objects on the ground. They respond to the strong electric field by growing positive streamers. These reach up anywhere between three and a few hundred feet above the ground. Finally, when a stepped leader and a positive streamer meet, the electric charge can drain to earth, resulting in the blinding flash of light we call lightning.

Wow! What an amazing picture!

For years, we have assumed that a lightning strike, which is a release of energy downwards from the huge static charge that has built up in the clouds, is just a one-way process – the cloud somehow determines where it's going to release its energy and Boom! It happens. Now we are discovering that the release of that static

---

[4] (https://www.youtube.com/watch?v=64WMsNRJvDo)

charge in the atmosphere is not automatic; the stepped leader descends towards the earth and it affects the atmosphere close to the earth, but it is looking for a response from the objects on the ground. It is looking for the "positive streamer," which looks like a long spark of electrical energy. It's like the positive streamer is saying, "I'm ready, pick me, pick me!"

The Lord began to show me that this is an amazingly accurate analogy of what has been happening in the Body of Christ. For years we have recognized the huge differential between the atmosphere in heaven and the atmosphere on earth. We've seen the occasional release of the power and atmosphere of heaven into the earthly realm, but we've known that it isn't enough – we have known that there's got to be more. And there is more! So we've prayed fervently for God to come through and bring "revival" into the earth, assuming that what we need, what the world needs now, is for God to show up and release His power and love into our community or nation. We've assumed that it's just a one-way process, but it's not.

God AND You

What the world needs now is not just God, but <u>God *and* you</u>, <u>God *and* me</u>! *It's the full blown mature relationship between God and His people that will bring the manifestation of heaven that people are longing for.*

God is looking for the "positive streamers" that will connect with the realm of heaven and bring a release of heaven's atmosphere into the earthly realm. While we don't yet understand everything about these positive streamers, we do know that lightning generally takes the path of *least resistance*. This is where the analogy develops further. What is the path of least resistance when it comes to heaven looking to manifest in the earth? I believe that *the path of least resistance is being in complete agreement with heaven* – regarding *who you are* and regarding *who God is*. I use the phrase "in agreement with heaven" deliberately. It's not just about being in agreement with God, because not only does God know who you are, but the angels know who you are, the elders know who you are, and the cloud of witnesses know who you are. All of heaven knows who you are! But do YOU know who you are?

Let's look at another hypothetical scenario – a relationship between two people. We'll call them Joe and Mary. They are married, they love each other very much, and they want their relationship to blossom and grow. They are building a culture of honor in their relationship; Mary regularly expresses to Joe his worth and value to her, and Joe continually expresses to Mary how he values her and celebrates the aspects of her character and personality as they are emerging. Then one day Mary gets to share her testimony at a home group and it really impacts the group. She shares naturally and with transparency about her journey in life, and the people can really relate to her. Joe is ecstatic! She's never done this before, and he encourages her and gives her really positive feedback as to how she came across to the group. But to Joe's dismay she doesn't receive his encouragement that well. She keeps responding by saying, "I don't really do that sort of thing very well. I was really nervous and I just made a fool of myself!" Joe counteracts this, saying that she really touched the group with what she shared, but she still won't receive what he's saying.

What's the problem? There is *resistance in her heart* to what Joe is saying because when she was a young girl, she had to give a talk in front of her class, and made a mistake while sharing. The class laughed at her, and afterwards one of her classmates told her that she was useless at speaking in front of others. That registered in her heart, and she came to believe that about herself. If Mary stays with that perception of herself and never does any more speaking in front of others, the relationship cannot fully blossom and grow because there's a part of Mary that is still shut down, and the gift that she so obviously has cannot develop and be a blessing to others. The problem is not that Joe is not honoring Mary – he is! The problem is that Mary is not able to receive Joe's honor of her because *she cannot come into agreement with him about what he sees in her.* Her heart is telling her something different because it has received a lie about her ability and embraced it as the truth. Whenever your heart believes something different than what your head believes, your heart will always win out. It is by far the more powerful of the two! That is why David says in Psalm 51:6, *"Behold, You desire truth in the innermost being, and in the hidden part You will make me know wisdom."*

DEALING WITH THE RESISTANCE

Let's take the relationship between Joe and Mary and change the names to – God and me. The scenario is the same. The biggest problem is not getting me to honor God. There will most likely be some changes I need to make in order to honor God well and express His worth consistently in my lifestyle, but I believe that by far the hardest thing is for me to receive, embrace, and respond to His honoring me, for me to come into agreement with what He says about me! For me to be impacted by the degree of joy that He has in me, for me to receive the revelation that He actually celebrates me and that He delights in who I am and in how He made me! For me to allow those parts of my heart that are in disagreement with what He says about me to be touched by the Holy Spirit, healed and recalibrated. If I don't allow Him to deal with those areas of disagreement I will be maintaining a resistance in my life which will not allow a full discharge of the atmosphere of heaven into my earthly sphere of influence.

Acknowledge Who You Are

Many of us have this warped idea of what humility is, and think that it is seeing ourselves as having not much value and not having much to offer. That couldn't be further from the truth! That is not humility, it is the height of arrogance! When God is consistently saying how awesome you are, and how proud He is of you, and you say to Him, "God, I appreciate that You are saying these nice things about me, but I actually know more than You do, and I say that I am not that great at all," that is totally arrogant. That is disagreement with heaven and will produce just the kind of resistance in you that the enemy is looking for. It will prevent you from becoming a "positive streamer" whom God can flow through to bring the atmosphere of heaven into the earth.

True humility is being in complete agreement with God – about who He is, about who you are, and about what you can do in relationship with Him. *Pride manifests itself when you try to take the credit for who you are.* When you acknowledge who you are AND give God the credit for it, you will stay in true humility, and that is a position that Satan truly fears.

Philemon 1:6 says, *"...I pray that the fellowship of your faith may become effective through the knowledge of every good thing which is in you for Christ's sake."* The word translated *fellowship* means "communication." Paul here is saying that the communication of our faith becomes effective through the knowledge [the recognition, full discernment and acknowledgement] of every good thing that is in us. The enemy is trying to shut you down on the inside and stunt your growth by persuading you that you shouldn't acknowledge what is in you, because that is pride. But God is saying, "No! Recognize what I've put within you. Acknowledge it as a gift from Me and celebrate who I've made you to be!" As you discover each good thing that He has put within you, acknowledge it, begin to use it, develop it, give it room to function and watch it grow!

We need you, and we need everything that God has put within you to be released in the earth in these days. You literally have come to the Kingdom for such a time as this! What would it look like for the real you to be revealed and released? Are there gifts and abilities you have that you haven't begun to utilize yet? Are there opportunities to serve others that you have been ignoring, because you think that you don't have what it takes? Are there books to be written, films to be made, inventions to be created that are sitting dormant within you? Is there life experience that you have that others could benefit from?

There is one person that you are likely to dishonor more than anyone else. Who? You!

Remember, when you dishonor someone, you shut yourself off from receiving who they really are, so part of the process of acknowledging who you are is to learn to honor yourself.

What are some ways you can do that?

- Make an honest evaluation of your strengths and weaknesses. Ask a trusted friend to help you with this.

- Permit yourself to say, "Yes I am good at..." (whatever the activity may be)

- Tap into the desires of your heart and ask yourself, "What are some things I would really like to do that would help others but I'm currently not doing them?"

- Invest some time and money in training that will help you develop some of the skill sets you have.

- Make sure that you are looking after yourself (not pampering yourself) by getting enough sleep, rest, good food, etc. You are definitely worth looking after!

- Adjust your self-talk, if necessary, and speak to yourself the positive things that God is saying about you.

What Is He Saying About You?

- He has crowned you with glory and honor. (Romans 8:29; Hebrews 2:7)

- He has given you the same exalted state as Jesus. (John 17:22)

- You are part of His family, with Jesus as your elder brother. (Hebrews 2:10)

- You have been invited to join in the same relationship with Father and Holy Spirit that Jesus has with them. (John 14:21,23; 17:23,25-26; Ephesians 2:19; Colossians 3:1-3)

- You are as high, positionally, as it is possible to be. (Psalm 91:14; Ephesians 2:4-6,19; Colossians 3:1-3)

- He is ecstatic about you, and wildly celebrates you! (Zephaniah 3:17)

- You are profoundly loved. (John 15:9; Romans 5:8; 8:35-39)

- He will not remind you of your past failures. (Zephaniah 3:17; Hebrews 8:12)

- You are totally forgiven of all your sins – past, present and future! (Hebrews 10:12,14,18; 1 John 1:9)

- You are righteous in His sight. (Romans 5:17; 2 Corinthians 5:21)

- You have access to His joy. (John 15:11)

- You have access to His peace. (John 14:27)

- You have access to His faith. (Galatians 2:20)

- You have access to His divine nature. (2 Peter 1:4)

- You are already qualified to be a minister – a waiter or waitress – of the Spirit. You aren't required to heal anybody or create a word of knowledge – you can't, just like it's not a waitress' responsibility to provide the meal. She just needs to talk to the customer, find out what they need, order it from the chef, and then pass it on to them. You are already qualified to do that in the realm of the Spirit! (2 Corinthians 3:6)

- You can pray for the sick and see them healed. (Matthew 10:8; Mark 16:18)

- You can receive God's heart for a person and share that with them – you can prophesy. (1 Corinthians 14:31)

- You can cast out demons. (Mark 16:17)

- You can speak in new tongues. (Mark 16:17

- You can do the things that Jesus did – and more. (John 14:12-13)

- You are a New Covenant priest. (1 Peter 2:5,9)

- You are a person with divine influence and your prayers are powerful. (James 5:16)

THE LIFE-GIVING POWER OF HONOR

Conclusion

Thank you for taking the time to read this book. I am on a journey, just like you, and although I have not yet entered into the fullness of who God created me to be, I am excited about the journey, and I want to keep moving forward in the grand adventure that He has called us to. There are realms of revelation and encounter with God that He is waiting for us to enter and experience. There are manifestations of His love and power that He says He has already qualified us to minister and dispense. Are you excited and challenged by this? I know I am!

Romans 8:14 tells us, *"For all who are being led by the Spirit of God, these are sons of God."* You are a child of God and He wants you to be led by Holy Spirit, your personal coach. As you ponder what you've been reading in these chapters, are there any things that you've read where you feel: "I must work on that in my life!" One of the things that the enemy will try to do is to take a right desire, the desire to please God, and twist it so that it becomes a self-imposed bondage that restricts you, rather than frees you. The enemy will try and tell you that God won't accept you unless you change, but it's too late! God already loves you and accepts you; so rather than working on things in your life in order to gain His love, work on them from the right foundation – the knowledge that you are already loved and celebrated.

The Holy Spirit is the divine catalyst in your relationship with Him – He is your personal coach and your greatest encourager! Don't try to change lots of things in your life at once. Ask Holy Spirit, "What are you wanting to highlight for me? What is our next step in the journey?" You are already loved, already celebrated, already totally accepted. So, out of that place of security, listen to what He tells you.

He may want to give you new eyes to see the people around you differently. He may want to show you where there are areas of disagreement in your heart to what God is saying about you. Are there any of these things that your heart finds difficult to embrace as being true for you personally? Why not talk to Him about them and let Him deal with the lies that you have come to believe about yourself, and ask Him to bring you into a revelation of truth – truth that will set you free and give you wings!

He may want to show you where you've unwittingly been letting attitudes or responses convey a value statement to God that is making it harder for Him to be Himself to you. But even with any of those things, I can guarantee that Holy Spirit will be shouting His approval of you, expressing Father's delight in you, and basically being His outrageously extravagant, encouraging, enthusiastic self – because that's what He's like!

You are totally free to be your unique self and we need you to be you – we need everything that you have, and everything that you are, expressed in the earth, just as we need God to be everything that He is amongst us.

I would love to hear how He's leading you in your grand adventure with Him. Feel free to email me at the email address listed on the "About the Author" page and let me know.

CONCLUSION

ooOoo

Reflection Points

- What would it look like for the real you to be revealed and released?

- Are there gifts and abilities that you have but you've not utilized yet?

- Are there opportunities to serve others that you have been ignoring, because you think you don't have what it takes?

- Think about the following statement – *"There is one person that you are likely to dishonor more than anyone else – you!"* How true is that statement in regard to your life? In what ways do you dishonor yourself? What things can you do to change that?

- Look through the list in this chapter of things that God is saying about you. Are there any of these things that your heart finds difficult to embrace as being true for you personally? Why do you think that is?

- What are some of the really great things about you that you can give thanks to God for? Recognizing them and acknowledging them is a really powerful thing to do. Celebrate who God has made you, and allow others to celebrate you, too!

Acknowledgements

There are so many people who have had a profound impact on my life and have helped me to grow in my walk with God over the years, and I am deeply indebted to each one. They are too numerous to mention here, but in particular I want to thank the following:

My wife Lyn – Thank you so much for your love, encouragement, passion for living, and your desire to help people discover their identity and live out of that. You are truly inspirational!

My children, Dan and Tanya, my daughter-in-law Aimee and my son-in-law Phil – You've charted your own course in life and it's been a pleasure watching you grow and discover the good things that God has put within you, then seeing you share them with the world. Thanks for all the fun times, outdoor adventures, game nights, family meals and times doing life together.

Patricia King – What an inspiration you are! God has truly given you eyes to see the best in people, to champion them in their journey and to help make room for them to flourish and grow. Your passionate love for God and for people has led you to model everything that I have discussed in this book, and more! Your lifestyle of honor has impacted my life immeasurably. Thank you so much!

Benji and Alanna Alexander, John and Fiona Steffens and the rest of the gang at Revival School Aotearoa New Zealand – Thank you for your partnership in exploring the awesomeness of life with Jesus together! Your passion for love, honor, integrity, transparency and the desire to lay hold of everything that God has made available to us has inspired and strengthened me beyond what words can describe! You are a living example of how an environment of honor releases people to be who they really are, and it's highly contagious!

Last, but not least – Father God, Jesus and Holy Spirit – Thank You for the invitation to become a part of Your family, for the experience of Your incredible love, for the passion that's in Your heart for each one of us, and for the awesome way that You are revealing Yourself to us in these days. My life will never be the same as a result of meeting You, and I know that the adventure You've called us to will never end!

About Rob Packer

Rob Packer is a man who lives the message contained in this book. To him, "honor" is not just a concept – it is a foundational value on which his life and ministry is built. He is a man who sees and believes the best in people, calling them into the fullness of their identity in Christ through his words, attitudes and actions.

For over forty years Rob has trained and equipped believers around the world, establishing strong foundations in their lives and empowering them to walk in their calling. He is a skilled communicator and gifted teacher, a widely respected "father in the faith," and mentor to many. His teaching has a clarity and practicality that enables people to easily grasp and put into practice what is being taught.

Rob is also a songwriter, worship leader, and music teacher with many years of experience in these areas. Because of his gifting and wisdom he has become a trusted mentor of many worship leaders.

He has produced numerous ministry resources, including training manuals, worship and soaking CDs, and DVDs.

Rob and his wife Lyn co-lead XP Ministries in New Zealand (under Patricia King's oversight) and they have also held senior pastoral positions in several New Zealand churches over their forty-plus years of ministry. Rob is also a part-time worship pastor at Hope Centre, their home church in Tauranga.

In his spare time Rob loves to get out on the ocean in his sea kayak and explore the coastline of his beautiful nation, or ride his bike and explore the various trails in the Bay of Plenty, the region he lives in.

For more information about Rob's teachings, to see his itinerary, or to invite him to minister to your church or group, go to XP Ministries New Zealand www.xpnewzealand.com or email him at nz@xpministries.com

www.ingramcontent.com/pod-product-compliance
Lightning Source LLC
Chambersburg PA
CBHW070109080526
44586CB00013B/1242